# Praise for *Let Go Now*

"Karen Casey teaches us how to row our boat (note: not other people's boats) gently down the stream. When we row gently, we don't yell who or what must be on the bank around the bend. We peacefully accept what comes and this makes us very merry. We quietly bless the people who are there, knowing that is exactly where they should be. We let go and allow the River to carry us home, certain that the River is our God-given will, our safety, our comfort, and our peace. *Let Go Now* is one of the most profoundly spiritual and helpful books I have read."

—**Hugh Prather**, author of *Morning Notes*
and *The Little Book of Letting Go*

"You just can't go wrong with Karen Casey. In *Let Go Now* she steers a course though the at-times confusing waters of detachment. She takes the reader though 200 little classes explaining what detachment is and what it is not. This book would help anyone trying to live a life as serene yet productive as possible in this often busy time."

—**Earnie Larsen**, author of *Stage II Recovery: Life
Beyond Addiction* and *From Anger to Forgiveness*

"A cornerstone concept of both Eastern philosophy and Twelve Step programs, detachment is often misunderstood and misapplied. In *Let Go Now* Karen Casey elegantly brings this time-honored term into everyday situations so that it can become a true, userfriendly tool for recovery. She not only tells us what detachment means, she shows us how to do it, one day at a time."

—**Tian Dayton**, PhD, author of *Emotional Sobriety:
From Relationship Trauma to Resilience and Balance*

T0124535

"Casey has given us a wonderful guidebook for one of life's ongoing challenges—detachment—so essential to our spiritual health. No one with a caring heart would want to miss this essential read. Another winner for Karen Casey and thus for all of us!"

—**Marilyn J. Mason**, PhD, author of *Igniting the Spirit at Work* and coauthor of *Facing Shame: Families in Recovery*

"My measure of a book's worth: 1. Does it open a window in my mind? 2. Do I change? 3. Is my life improved? The answer? Yes on all counts for *Let Go Now.*"

—**Anne Katherine**, author of *Boundaries and Lick It!*

# LET GO NOW

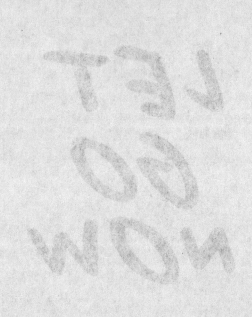

# LET GO NOW

## EMBRACE DETACHMENT AS A PATH TO FREEDOM

## KAREN CASEY

### Conari Press
Coral Gables, FL

Cover Morgane Leoni
Layout & Design: Maxine Ressler
Birds Illustration: andrei / Adobe Stock

For permission requests, please contact the publisher at:
Mango Publishing Group
2850 S Douglas Road, 4th Floor
Coral Gables, FL 33134 USA
info@mango.bz

For special orders, quantity sales, course adoptions and corporate sales, please email the publisher at sales@mango.bz. For trade and wholesale sales, please contact Ingram Publisher Services at customer.service@ingramcontent.com or +1.800.509.4887.

Let Go Now: Embrace Detachment as a Path to Freedom

Library of Congress Cataloging-in-Publication Data: 2022934388
ISBN: (print) 978-1-64250-447-7 (ebook) 978-1-64250-448-4
BISAC: OCC019000, BODY, MIND & SPIRIT / Inspiration & Personal Growth

I DEDICATE THIS BOOK TO MY HUSBAND, JOE, A WONDERFUL companion and "teacher" who makes my journey fun every day. He eases the rough spots without my even asking. I am so blessed.

# Contents

**pause** *and* **reflect** *54*

**pause** *and* **reflect** *65*

81. Detachment from others can be nurtured by strengthening our "attachment" to our personal hopes and dreams. *99*

82. Detachment is not interfering with what another person should do. *100*

83. Detachment is refusing to let our interactions with others define us. *101*

84. Detachment means no longer needing to be in charge of anything, not even our own lives. *102*

85. Detachment is not disinterest, but that might be the first step. *103*

86. Detachment means no longer leading others' lives. *104*

87. Detachment is respecting the boundaries between yourself and others. *105*

88. Detachment is freedom from the desire to get someone back. *106*

89. Detachment is the freedom not to be angry or sad. *107*

90. Detachment is giving up control, even the thought of it! *108*

91. Detachment is not letting anyone else decide how you feel. *110*

92. Detachment is freedom from saying, "I told you so." *111*

93. Detachment is being able to put yourself at the top of the list of "who needs care." *112*

94. Detachment is letting our friends have whatever kind of day they choose to have. *113*

95. Detachment means acknowledging and even celebrating another's unique journey. *114*

96. Detachment is no longer "dancing" around someone else's life. *115*

97. Detachment is no longer needing to assuage anyone else's anger. *116*

98. Detachment is being able to claim our own identities. *117*

99. Detachment is accepting what we cannot change and changing only what we can. *118*

100. Detachment is not taking anyone else's behavior personally. *119*

180: Detaching from the chaos of others' lives may
    not look like love, but it is. *207*

### pause *and* reflect *208*

181: Detaching from our friends spurs some of them on
    to being more responsible. *209*

182: A sure indication that we have not embraced detachment
    is when our focus is too much on someone else. *210*

183: Detachment doesn't have to mean disinterest. *211*

184: Accepting detachment as a loving act seems strange to some. *212*

185: Surrendering your control over life, your own life and the lives
    of others, is a great demonstration of detachment. *213*

186: Our willingness to detach from others is enhanced if
    we have developed trust in a Higher Power. *214*

187: Detachment can feel like lack of love. But it's really God's will. *215*

188: Dreams can help us in our development of any skill.
    Detachment is one of them. *216*

189: Making the commitment to detach from our loved ones
    (and all others too) is a big change for many of us. *217*

190: Being willing to practice the art of detachment is
    what promises us the freedom to grow. *218*

### pause *and* reflect *219*

191: Embracing silence in the face of turmoil
    is an act of detachment. *220*

192: Sharing a path in life doesn't mean stepping
    on each other's toes. *221*

193: Our greatest asset in life is having God's presence, whether it's
    to help us detach from others or simply to breathe. *222*

194: The recognition of another person's need for space helps us develop
    our own commitment to the healing value of detachment. *223*

195: Sometimes we resist detaching from the problems of
    others because reacting feels so good. *224*

196: If we want freedom from our addiction to controlling others,
    prayer is the solution, and detachment is the result. *225*

197: The art of detachment is best learned by watching our teachers. *226*

# Foreword

Seven years ago, I walked—actually reluctantly fell—into the rooms of Al-Anon. Like so many looking for answers to this baffling and horrible disease, I too wanted guidance. My precious daughter is an alcoholic, and I was exhausted trying to find ways to help her, protect her, relieve her from her suffering. In those rooms, I heard for the first time the concept of detaching with love—letting go. Are you kidding? I had spent over thirty-five years being close to my daughters, involved and engaged in their lives, caring about every aspect of their living. How could "letting go" of them be the loving, right thing to do? I didn't know how to begin to "let go." I wasn't even sure if "letting go" was what we needed, but I was willing to look at something different even though it was opposite of the way I had always parented. So I went to the bookstore and asked to be directed to books on alcoholism, recovery, and detachment. A young woman guided me to a rather large section of self-help books, and I started perusing them. My hand landed on a book titled *Let Go Now*. I don't know if it was the word *now* or the endorsement on the back from *Publishers Weekly* saying, "An easy reference guide for those seeking recovery or peace." I took it home and started reading it that night. This book has been by my bedside for three years—just seeing the title when waking up from a nightmare gives me the immediate direction needed: "Let Go Now." I will quietly grab the book, steal away to the bathroom so I can turn on a light, and read a meditation. It slowly walks me back from that place of panic where I'm projecting the worst-case scenario and feeling the responsibility to fix something that isn't mine to fix, reminding me to let go, and to do it this very moment, in this present moment of NOW.

I've read this book a dozen times since it has taken residence on my nightstand. Each time I read it, I feel like I'm reading it for the first time. I have to believe this is a spiritual connection from Karen's heart to mine even though her intent is to release a spiritual expression to whoever wants to receive it. I'm so grateful, so thankful, that my Great Spirit has placed me in the position to be the recipient of the love that slowly works its way to the wisdom and freedom of *Let Go Now.*

—Siouxzy Murphy

# Preface

When *Let Go Now* was first published over a decade ago, it felt like one of the most important of all the books I had ever written. And it still feels that way! Each and every one of the thoughts included in these pages continues to ring true.

I am inclined to think it's because the simple suggestion to "let go now"—of the behavior, the dreams and aspirations, and especially the opinions of others, continues to be an idea that I need to embrace. It takes practice. Daily.

Minding the business of others simply comes naturally, at least to some of us. A very good friend of mine often says, "there are two kinds of business: my business and none of my business." Although this is a clever comment, its wisdom is profound. Letting others conduct the business of their lives without our interference is a wise and mighty choice, one that's good for all parties.

Detachment doesn't mean dissolution of any relationship, unless it's intentional. Nor does it mean absence of love or kindness. Detachment is allowing ourselves and anyone close to us to be **as they are**, without our interference. In other words, to kindly and gently detach from their journey, allowing them to find their own way while we travel our own path, too. I've come to believe that to let go and embrace detachment is the kindest, most loving thing we can do. It is the purest form of love that I know.

Letting go isn't all that easy. The tensions so easily observed between friends, colleagues, family members, and even between perfect strangers suggest this. But it's important, especially in times of chaos and strife, fear and uncertainty. The ability to let go just may be one of the most important things any one of us can do to improve the condition of our daily lives.

To live and let live—that is our assignment. When we practice this, we will know peace. And those we let go of may just discover a glimmering of peace, too. That may be the sweetest gift of all.

I wrote this book for you and for me, too. My inner voice guides every word I write and I am comforted by this thought. How lucky for both of us.

May our paths continue to cross.

Karen Casey

# Introduction

HOW DO WE *EMBRACE* DETACHMENT? WHY SHOULD WE even want to? Those are questions that prompted my desire to write this book. *Detachment,* according to the dictionary, means "separation." *Embrace* means "to come together." How can we do both in the same moment?

It's my intention to make this conundrum clear as you move through this book. In the meditations you will come to understand not only the necessity for "loving" detachment within our many relationships—those that are dear to us as well as those that cause us concern—but also the importance of embracing this concept if you want a peaceful journey through life.

To begin with, I think we have to cultivate our willingness to let go, that is, to detach from the trials and tribulations of our contemporaries if we want to find the quiet peace we long for, a peace that will allow us to truly love, to truly embrace, and to appreciate those who journey with us. In this process, we also give those companions the freedom to grow and to find their own way, thus their own eventual peace too. I don't think we can come together as loving equals without *embracing* the willingness to detach.

We live very codependent lives, from my perspective. By this I mean that too many of us let even the whims of others—in our families, our communities, our workplaces, even in other parts of the world—define us, determine how we feel, and then decide what we will do next in many instances. Learning to detach allows us to live the life we were meant to live. By allowing other people's behavior, good, bad, or *disinterested,* control us, we miss many opportunities for movement and expression in new directions. The converse is also true: if we attempt to control the other persons on our path, wherever they may reside, keeping them "attached" to us through any means (and most of us are very practiced at this), we immobilize them, thus preventing the growth they deserve and have been prepared for already.

Detachment isn't easy. If it were, there would be no need for a book offering to help you develop the skills to do it. And it may not have appeared on your radar screen as something you wanted to cultivate prior to picking up this book. As was already noted, we are accustomed to being enmeshed with others, letting our lives be constantly influenced by their behavior. I am not suggesting that this influence is always bad; there are good influences too, probably everyday. We can and do observe healthy "detached" behavior in some of our friends, and perhaps they showed up on our path to serve as our teachers. It's not always easy to discern the "good" from the "bad," however. It's my intent for the meditations here to illustrate those behaviors we want to mimic and those we don't.

It is my hope that this book, *Let Go Now: Embrace Detachment as a Path to Freedom*, will clarify many of your questions about detachment: what it is, how to do it, and how to practice it with others. It's also my hope that you will give yourself all the time you need to fully absorb the concepts and to develop the skills as outlined. I didn't come to appreciate the value of detachment easily, and the idea of embracing it came even later. But the peaceful tenor of my journey today is surely the result of my commitment to practicing and "embracing" detachment at every opportunity.

I believe that every moment of our lives is offering us just such an opportunity. And wherever we are, others are on hand to observe, to reap the benefit of our "practice," and to carry what they have seen into their own lives.

## How to Use this Book

After reading my story about detachment, about how and why I came to realize I needed help and about the transformation that has happened in my life, turn to the meditations. Don't read them quickly or all at once. Savor them. Meditate on them. Read one a day or spread one of them over a two- or three-day period. There really is no hurry. It's a practice that actually has no ending point. Or use the subject index at the back of the book if you feel the need to zero in on a specific topic for your well-being on a particular day. What I am suggesting is this: there is no one way, no right way, to use this book. It's yours to use in whatever way makes the most sense for you. Only you and your Higher Power know what's best for you.

As you move through the book, you will note that following every ten meditations is a page for pausing and reflecting. At these points I suggest you get a journal and share your thoughts, as triggered by my comments, for your own growing success with this ever-so-important skill, a skill that, if mastered, I promise will change every moment of the rest of your life.

You will also note that I have repeated myriad times many of the specific ideas from various perspectives. That's very intentional. If you are like me, it takes more than one explanation, more than one reading, to grasp a new idea. I think these ideas are important enough that they bear repeating.

Good luck with this book. You, and those you travel with, will benefit by all that you accomplish. Blessings to you on your journey.

## My Story

I want to begin with my own story as an illustration of what it was like before I understood detachment, what happened, and what it's like now that I am committed to the practice of detachment on a daily basis. My journey has been quite miraculous, I think, but what happened to me is certainly attainable by others. Anyone who is imprisoned by codependence, by "attachment" to others, will be able to relate. What I want all people to know is that life can become all that you want it to be, all that you dreamed of at some earlier time in your life. It certainly is not possible that what I learned was for my sole edification.

As a young girl growing up in a dysfunctional family, I became very skilled at reading the body language of others to see if I was "okay." I didn't get many signs of approval. My parents struggled in their relationship, and my dad's anger, coupled with my mom's sadness, permeated the household. I tiptoed around the rage when possible, and then as I got older, I raged too.

At age thirteen, I discovered the marvelous effects of alcohol from a glass of Coke spiked with whiskey that I surreptitiously mixed at a family wedding reception. From that day until May 24, 1976, I used alcohol to change the way my life looked and felt. But between the first drink and the last, some twenty-three years later, I was to undergo many traumas. The majority of them were complicated by my dependence on men, right along with my dependence on alcohol and other drugs.

I simply had mastered my ability to read another's every mood, and that became my mood too. I was soon imprisoned by the behaviors of others, and then I tried to control those behaviors, which I was sure was possible and, furthermore, would allow me to feel okay about myself and the relationship. Alas, it was not possible. My sense of isolation escalated and my grip on alcohol tightened.

Not surprising, my first marriage ended, one that I had been sure would provide me with the security I sought. Neither of us understood the effects of the alcohol on our lives. I didn't choose to see the effects even then and instead sought other relationships that also had alcohol as the glue. One relationship followed another, none of them mirroring the dream I had crafted for myself. But all the relationships had one thing in common: my inability to allow the other person to have a life of his own; thus, I had no real life either. I clung and harped and cried and used alcohol to feed the dark hole inside me.

Then I was introduced to Al-Anon, where the miracle actually began. I didn't very readily get the message being conveyed, but the joy I observed drew me back, week after week. I knew I wanted what the others in that room seemed to have, and they kept saying, "Keep coming back." I did, contentedly so. Eventually I began couple's counseling with my "significant other," a man who never once had time to come to our sessions. This should have been a red flag, but I simply didn't want to acknowledge what I suspected it meant.

The counselor eventually sought to hear my story anyway and sent me straight to Alcoholics Anonymous. It was there that my life got both better and worse. My dependence on men, any man, seemed like the solution to me. Even though I wasn't us= ing alcohol anymore to fill the dark hole, I was relying on the attention of men to have the same effect. The emotional insanity was crippling.

Because I was still going to Al=Anon, I was trying to man= age my feelings around others, but my success was limited. And then my sponsor said, "Stay out of relationships with men for a year and find out who you are, Karen." I complied, not very happily at first, but her words rang true. I still didn't cotton to most of the suggestions I was hearing in either Al=Anon or AA, but eventually my willingness grew. All I knew for sure was that others in the group knew more than I did, and I wanted what many of them had.

Being told that my life did not need to revolve around the moods, the actions, the dreams, the failures, or the successes of anyone else was information I simply didn't know how to ab= sorb. I had always "danced" around others; I knew no other dance. For quite a spell, I was at a loss, sitting on the sidelines. But then the messages I was hearing began to penetrate. I was "enough," they said; I didn't need the approval of anyone else. I had a God in whom I could trust to guide my every action, a God who loved me, flaws and all.

Then the messages, the principles that ultimately led to my grip on the meaning of detachment, thankfully multiplied:

> Wherever we are, God is present.
> Whoever comes our way is part of our learning curve.
> We have the power to change how we think.
> Appreciating the journey of everyone else is what gives my
>    own journey purpose.
> Peaceful feelings follow peaceful actions.
> The chaos of others need not attract us.
> No argument demands our participation.

Acting, rather than reacting, is blissful. To witness another's
   journey is all we are ever called to do.
Our teachers are everywhere. Silence may be the best
   response we can make in myriad situations.
There are two kinds of business: your business and none of
   your business.
Taking no hostages is the surest way to peace.

I have hung on to every one of these messages for dear life
at one time or another, and to many more that I illustrate in the
meditations that follow. They each became part of my lifeline
to sanity. They still are part of my lifeline. My understanding
of detachment and its value as the way to a peaceful heart and
journey is encased in each and every one of them. For more
than thirty years, I have worked to master these principles. I
have been more successful with some than with others. But my
journey is not finished. That's the great news I celebrate every
day when I wake up.

I have all the time I need to seek and enjoy the fruits of this
journey. Willingness comes first. Application of the principles
comes next. And gratitude to God and the hovering angels for
helping me is never to be forgotten. What any one of us does
today pays forward in someone's life tomorrow. And we are an
interconnected whole: whomever we help by our actions in this
moment will be available to help others tomorrow. I have loved
claiming my small part in the unending circle of peaceful living.
You can claim your part too. The world will be made better by
the efforts of all of us.

# meditations

Detachment is simply watching the events that are unfolding around you, getting involved *only* when your journey is part of the experience.

NOT REACTING TO THE PEOPLE OR THE SITUATIONS THAT so easily attract our attention is not an easy skill to develop. And a skill it is. We must practice driving and chipping and putting a golf ball in order to be good golfers. We have to hit thousands of tennis balls against a backdrop to play tennis competitively. And we have to sit for long, long hours at the piano keys in order to become proficient pianists. We would not expect to be very good at any one of these activities without practice—lots of it.

But we seldom grasp, until after many failures, sometimes years of failures, that we have to practice and rehearse again and again the "art" of not reacting, of "detaching," from the actions of those around us. How often we hear or, worse yet, say, "He made me do it!" Wrong! No one can make us do anything. Only we have the power to do or not do whatever we do. That's the good news, in fact. We are in charge of ourselves; no one else is. The freedom that accompanies this realization will lift our spirits throughout the day.

✦

Getting involved in the actions of others isn't in my best interests, most of the time. I will walk away when I need to today.

Detachment is stepping back from
an experience in order to allow room
for God to do His or Her part.

I SELDOM REMEMBER, WITHOUT SOME PRODDING THAT I initially resist, that God is a factor in every person's experience. My ego's first inclination is to think that I am a necessary factor—not just an ordinary necessary factor but the deciding one—in the lives of my friends and family. Giving up control and letting God be the key influence in the lives of my loved ones is not easy. It takes trust. Not only trust in God but also trust in others and in my own willingness to approach my experiences with all of them differently.

The benefit of coming to believe that God is the key factor in everyone's life is that it releases us from a heavy burden. Too many of us have tried to manage the lives of too many others for far too long. No one gains in that scenario. On the contrary, everyone loses the peace that comes with turning our lives over to the care and guidance of a loving God.

◆

Keeping a mental note of all the times I step away from
an experience that isn't mine to control will fill me with
a sense of empowerment. What a great opportunity this
will be today.

CHOOSING CONTENTMENT OVER AGITATION SEEMS LIKE a simple choice, but it apparently isn't for many of us. All we have to do is take a brief inventory of the many encounters we had yesterday. How many of them were peaceful? Did we take "the high road" very often? Were a few of those encounters riddled with words or actions that embarrass us in retrospect? Were there some we regret yet today?

It's been my experience that the encounters that are not peaceful fall into two categories: First, there are those that are the direct result of my trying to make something my business that is not my business—in other words, of my trying to control that which is not mine to control. The other category can best be described as letting someone else's behavior determine how I feel about myself. This becomes a cesspool, and I have wallowed in it far too many times. Fortunately, I am learning to make better choices. Now, I can walk away, most of the time, when I need to. How about you?

✦

The first few times we make the choice to "be peaceful rather than right," it feels like denial. But with practice it will become the preferred choice. Give it a try today.

## Detachment is making no one a project.

IT'S MY GUESS THAT SINCE YOU HAVE FOUND THIS BOOK of interest, you are able to relate to some of the struggles I have had over the years. One of these is "dancing around" the life of someone else, rather than leading my own life. I am pleased to say I have made a lot of progress in this arena, but for many decades, I didn't know there was any other way to live. If someone else wasn't at the center of my life, I wasn't sure who I was. What a sad existence. What a sad recollection, too.

Not letting someone else determine who we are or what we think or how we feel is revelatory when first encountered as an idea. I was introduced to this notion in 1971 in a book titled *Why Am I Afraid to Tell You Who I Am?* by John Powell. I immediately embraced the philosophy even though I knew it was a truth I was not yet able to practice. Now, many years later, I realize that we are often given the seed of an idea long before it's able to sprout real growth in our own lives. The fortunate thing is that we are never the same after the idea first presents itself.

◆

I am my only project! Fully embracing this idea gives me so much freedom to do the many things I have been born to do. Others are in our lives for a reason, but they are not present as our works in progress.

Detachment means taking no hostages.

5

PERHAPS YOU HAVE NEVER THOUGHT THAT YOUR OBSES-
sion with another person might be defined as hostage taking.
Historically, we think of hostages as those people who are imprisoned, particularly in a time of war. However, we can slide
quite easily into making a friend or loved one a hostage of sorts
by our attempts to control their every move. Our smothering
focus can be likened to making them our prisoner. But since the
natural inclination of every prisoner is to want to flee, the outcome of our behavior will never give us the result we are seeking.

Why is it that we are so determined to control someone else?
I have given this a lot of consideration for the past few years and
have concluded that our need to control others grows out of our
own insecurity. We fear abandonment, perhaps, or simple rejection at least. Both will become the reality if we insist on keeping
our focus on them rather than on us. Making the decision to
change our focus is an available option.

◆

While having a hostage might make us feel momentarily
secure, we can always expect them to try to escape. That's
the natural inclination. Is that really how we want to live?

15

PERHAPS YOU HAVE HEARD THIS WISE PHRASE: *OUR JOB is the effort, not the outcome.* But how often do we embrace it fully? Generally, we want to secure the result that we have imagined is the perfect one. To do this, we assume that we have to shepherd the project or the situation or the person down the path that leads to our definition of the "natural conclusion." But the correct conclusion—God's will—might not even resemble our will. That's not an easy adjustment to make in our thinking.

Hindsight is so revealing. For just a moment, recall a situation in your past that you were determined to control, but the outcome was simply not what you had envisioned. Can you see how much better God's outcome was? In my life, had I managed to make happen many of my "educated" choices, I'd not be alive to write this book. Thank goodness my Higher Power had a far better outcome for me than my own. Now I know, even though I am still inclined to forget, that doing my part and then letting go of the rest will ensure, at the very least, my peace of mind. I like that feeling.

✦

Detaching from outcomes, those that apply to us and those that apply to the actions of others, is the surest way to a peaceful day. Trying is believing.

## Detachment is letting the solutions be determined by God.

SOLUTIONS ARE SELDOM SIMPLE. PERHAPS THAT'S BECAUSE they generally involve other people too. When any one of us is certain that we have the best solution for any problem or situation confronting us, we have quite naturally chosen one that benefits us. There's nothing wrong with that stance. However, it may not be the best solution for all the people who are affected by the situation. Backing off and letting God be a participant in every decision results in an outcome that offers us peace of mind and the most beneficial solution for all.

If only we could remember that our Higher Power is a willing participant, we might call Him or Her the troubleshooter for every situation we encounter. We don't ever have to figure out anything alone. God would prefer otherwise, in fact. We need not ever make plans without consultation with the One who always knows the best direction for us to take. Our Higher Power is like having a GPS at our constant disposal that will, without fail, get us to our right destination. Always. And we can enjoy peace of mind. Always.

✦

Giving detachment a chance today will be like getting a paid vacation. We don't need to attend to situations that belong to others, and we can let God be part of every situation that does involve us. What relief we will feel.

# 8
Detachment is understanding that we are never the cause of someone else's actions.

WE LIVE IN A SOCIETY THAT WANTS TO BLAME OTHERS FOR every unfortunate situation that befalls us. Taking responsibility for the experiences we have, particularly when they are unpleasant, is not behavior that comes naturally to us. Most of us likely pattern our ideas and attitudes after those we observed in our homes. Our parents mimicked their parents too, no doubt, so this habit has had a long life. It controls how most of us see and think and behave. It also has colored the attitudes of the people with whom we are sharing our journey. But it's time to stop this merry-go-round of blame.

No one can cause us to act in a particular way, and *we are not to blame for anyone else's actions either!* Others' actions are theirs, and solely theirs. Likewise, our choices about how to behave are ours. We might influence others or even be influenced, but the final decision about how one acts falls with the one acting. We may not be all too happy about taking full responsibility for ourselves in every instance, nor in relinquishing the responsibility for how others behave. But we will grow accustomed to this, and it will free us from many burdens. Time will prove this to be true.

◆

Not having to be responsible for anyone but ourselves is a new way of seeing for many of us. Today can be peace-filled if we revel in this understanding.

THE INSANITY OF HANGING ON TO THOSE SITUATIONS OR recollections that disturbed our well-being, sometimes of occurrences that happened years ago, thinking that if we just figure them out we can change the people or the outcome, is far too familiar. I speak from experience! How often I have let the behavior of others take control of my emotions or my actions. My memories of a past slight, or an imagined slight, can easily be conjured up, and my feelings can be hurt or I can feel angry all over again. How embarrassing to admit this after all the years I have been making this spiritual journey. But alas, it's true, and I think it may occasionally be true for others, too.

This is not about living perfectly. It's about making progress, even a bit of progress, as regularly as possible. My struggle with acceptance has been the big issue lately. I simply have forgotten that it's not my job to change others or to even expect others to change. My job is to accept people as they are, knowing that their journey is exactly as it needs to be for them, as is mine. We are always where we need to be on this path. We are always traveling with those we need to travel with. Period. There are no accidents. Ever.

◆

I will accept whatever is happening as part of the plan for me today. With God's help I can be fully accepting.

Detachment frees up our time.

WHEN WE ARE INVOLVED IN THE PLANS, THE PROBLEMS, the details, and the actions of others, whether friend, spouse, or child, we have less time to attend to our own lives. Many of us think that part of our "assignment" here is being available to whomever and whatever their focus is. But that's not true, not ever true, in fact. As parents we may need to closely supervise the activities of our children, but we shouldn't limit our focus to that alone. Our lives are, or can be, much richer than our role as parent or spouse or friend. Our attention must remain on those things that have "called to us" and only us on our journey.

Perhaps detachment was an unfamiliar concept to you before picking up this book. When I first heard the word, I struggled to understand its meaning. I deciphered it by going through the door of "attachment," actually. I did know how it felt to be attached to someone else. I had tried to keep loved ones attached to me for years. Coming to see that detachment was letting go, releasing others to make their own choices, their own mistakes, to realize their own dreams, initially felt like loneliness to me. My life simply had been a dance around others. Letting them be meant I was dancing alone. But then I discovered the freedom I had to actually move in ways that pleasured me, and joy replaced the tension that had haunted me for years. At last.

◆

There will always be enough time to do what I am being called to do when I keep my attention where it belongs—on me.

# pause *and* reflect

To detach is not unloving.
It's giving space to our loved ones to grow.
It's the kindest gift we can give a friend.
It's the kindest gift we can give to ourselves.

Think of some situations over the past few days in which you successfully "freed someone from your hold on them." Journal for a few minutes to strengthen your resolve.

Think of your own feeling of freedom when you let go. What did it feel like? Are you committed to seeking more of this feeling? Journal about the growth you seek and the growth you have already attained with "letting go."

CLOSELY MONITORING ONE LIFE IS REALLY QUITE ENOUGH. Paying too close attention to someone else's life will only upset the balance of our own. We have the energy to live one life, not two or more. It's God's work to orchestrate the lives of others. Why are we so insistent on taking on more than we have been selected to do? Could it be that we are afraid others will leave us behind if we aren't wrapped up in their plans, their daily activities, their dreams for the future?

Having a simpler life, one that concerns itself with only our activities, is really so refreshing. So energizing. So peaceful. Until we remove our attention from the machinations of others, we can't even get a sense of what having more energy, extended periods of peace, and the joy that comes with detachment feels like. But once we have allowed ourselves to know this feeling, we will hunger for it more and more. In time, we will seek the freedom of detachment on a daily basis. And on a daily basis we will live peacefully.

✦

Being peaceful and enjoying the simple life doesn't have to elude us. Keeping our focus where it belongs is the method for attaining this peace. Today is the right day to seek it.

OBSESSION WITH THE ACTIONS OF OTHERS—WISHING they would change, wanting more attention or perhaps less, wishing our significant others would let us decide their fate—is so exhausting. When we are caught up in the cycle of obsession, we are seldom even aware of how we are letting our own lives slip away. But slip away they will. Learning how to let go of others and their lives takes willingness, a tremendous commitment to staying the course, and constant practice. If we don't keep this as a goal for our lives, we will miss the opportunities God is sending us for our own unique growth. We can only do justice to one life; ours.

Being detached from someone does not mean no longer caring for them. It does not mean pretending they no longer exist. It does not mean avoiding all contact with them. Being detached simply means not letting their behavior determine our feelings. It means not letting their behavior determine how we act, how we think, how we pray. Detachment is a loving act for all concerned. No one wants to be the constant center of someone else's life, at least not for long. Two people lose their lives when either one is constantly focused on the other. That's not why we are here.

✦

We can journey together today. From the shared journey we learn. But being enmeshed with another rather than complementing another's journey will destroy both parties. I will keep this in my memory bank today.

I, FOR ONE, AM ALL TOO FAMILIAR WITH HOW OBSESSING over the actions of others can cause my emotions to spin out of control. Left unchecked, I can find myself in a downward spiral that feels overwhelming and can lead to the awful feeling of hopelessness that used to be a constant companion. Obsession with others on our path can creep up on us when least expected. But I have come to understand, with the help of those wiser than myself on this journey, that when I am not staying close enough to my Higher Power, I am very vulnerable to the old habit of watching others and letting how they behave determine how I feel.

I have been on this spiritual journey for many decades, actually for my whole life when I acknowledge that God was always present even when I was unable to acknowledge it. And yet, I can slip away from the very habits that keep me serene, sane, and living in the joy that is my birthright. I am quite certain the same is true for many of you. We can learn how to detach. We can think about God rather than about what someone else is doing or not doing. Moving our thoughts from one to the other is the key to happiness. It's guaranteed.

✦

Being lovingly detached is the best way to honor one another's journey. Everyone is here for a specific set of lessons. We must allow everyone to follow his or her own inner guidance to learn their lessons.

Detachment is knowing that what
others do is not a reflection on you.

14

WHEN OUR COMPANIONS ACT OUT OR TREAT US POORLY
in public, when our friends or partners are rude or ill-behaved in
any way, it's easy to think that others are judging us along with
our partner for whatever they have done, particularly if we have
been guilty of this form of judgment ourselves. I don't think we
instinctively know that another person's behavior reflects solely
on them, never on us. If others do judge us for someone else's
behavior, it's generally because they are enmeshed in the actions
of others themselves.

Having good boundaries with the people on our journey
requires daily attention. Because we know others are sharing our
journey for the lessons we are both here to learn, it's easy to slip
over the line that actually separates what any one of us individually needs to master. We aren't separate from one another in the
spiritual sense, but that's another matter. Let's not confuse the
two. When we do, *others'* actions and choices get in the way of
*your* peace of mind. And neither of us can find the joy that has
been promised us.

◆

Defining our boundaries with others serves both of us. It
assures us that we will never get entrapped in emotions that
belong to someone else.

## 15   Detachment is not making a big deal of situations, even complicated ones.

WHEN I WAS WHINING FOR THE UMPTEENTH TIME ABOUT a situation over which I had no control, a good friend said, "So what?" I was initially startled, miffed, and even slightly hurt, but soon realized that she had done me a great service. I was creating a drama over a very minor, though often repeated, situation. And the reality is, we don't need to dramatize even major situations. When we allow God into the mix of the resolution, calm can prevail. As I have matured, calm has become far more attractive to me.

Knowing that "I can feel peace instead of this" has been a lifesaving mantra. The only problem is that I have to remember to use it. Periodically I slide into old behavior and let what's happening around me influence how I am feeling. When my emotions get triggered by what I am seeing others do or hearing what others are saying, I have given up my own life for the moment. Their actions or words may not make me angry, but they can create my reality for that moment. With practice, I can remember to create my own reality, and I'm far better for it.

+

Creating my own reality is an excellent undertaking every moment of the day. Unless I am in the flow of detaching from others, my reality will be clouded by their behavior.

THE GIFT OF EMPOWERMENT COMES EVERY TIME WE LET someone else decide his or her fate. Even the tiny decision someone might be struggling with doesn't need our input unless asked for. This is not an easy realization to come to grips with. So much of our persona may well be tied to having our friends or family members mirror our choices. And yet, when we lay that expectation on them or simply hold that expectation quietly within, we will experience chaos. No one wants to be controlled. Even when we are subtle about it, it's recognized and resisted.

You may be wondering what empowerment feels like if this is a new concept to you. It's probably best understood in terms of synonyms. It's freedom. It's peace of mind. It's not feeling absorbed by the antics of others. It's clarity of thinking. It's a feeling of lightness throughout the body. It's having the time to be joyful and unencumbered. It's having the sense that our Higher Power is close. Detachment is truly a gift of great proportions. Nothing can be well attended to when our emotions are attached to the actions of others.

♦

**Today I will become willing to let God, not my companions, be the center of my life.**

OVERREACTING TO THE MYRIAD SITUATIONS IN MY LIFE, whether bona fide major ones or extremely minor incidents, was once standard practice. Maybe you can relate. It made little difference what my spouse or a friend or co-worker did; I was capable of taking their actions or words quite personally and then acting in ways that were seldom fitting for the situation. The idea of considering how *I* wanted to respond and then actually responding in a sane way had never occurred to me. For decades I had watched my family of origin react to whatever happened, and I was a great imitator.

Learning that there is *another way* to see, to interpret, to respond is like being given a second chance at life. We are on this path with others because of what we each have to learn. We are journeying together. *Intentionally.* We are not making the journey for each other or as each other. Doing for others what they need to do for themselves prevents the learning that needs to occur, both ours and theirs. Stepping aside and watching others handle that which is theirs to handle, and not letting what they do determine how we feel, is the "real stuff" of this journey. Discovering this makes every minute pretty exciting.

◆

Making the decision to thoroughly enjoy this or any other day is pretty simple. It relies on our willingness to not let the actions of others take over our minds. We are in charge of what we think, what we say, what we do. Grabbing hold of this principle will change everything.

DO NOTHING. WHAT A CONCEPT. WITH WHAT FREQUENCY does your mind savor the idea of doing nothing when a partner or friend pushes your buttons? Probably not very often, unless you have already acquired some understanding of the pitfalls of being too attached to the whims, the behavior, or the attitudes and opinions of others. Simply walking away when our ego really wants to scream in retaliation is not easy. In fact, it may feel nearly impossible. But it can be done. I know; I have learned to do it.

Not responding—in other words, detaching—doesn't mean we don't care what the other person is doing or saying to or about us. We may care a great deal. But we have to ask ourselves, Will it help this situation for me to say something? If it honestly will, try to speak lovingly; but in most instances, letting the moment pass will be more fruitful. Adding fuel to the embers of an ugly incident will cause it to erupt into flames that can easily get out of control. We have all been there. We don't ever have to go there again.

◆

Making the choice to do nothing when we feel like someone is trying to egg us on is a hugely important decision. The empowerment we will feel is so worth the effort it takes to simply let the moment pass.

THE URGE TO RESPOND VERBALLY, AND GENERALLY NOT TOO kindly, to a perceived attack, an imagined affront, or an unmistakable put-down is overwhelming sometimes. Although giving in to the urge is not the end of the world, it will not help the situation. In most instances, the solution to a situation that borders on ugly is to bless it and let it go. Those who attack us in any form are full of fear. It may be fear of lack of control, fear of not getting what they deserve, fear of rejection, or fear of looking insignificant that makes them do and say what injures others. But certainly fear is at the root.

Saying to ourselves in those situations that no harm is meant will defuse the emotions that might be running through our mind at that time. Responding from an angry place, whether seemingly justified or not, will not make for a productive resolution. The only sensible response to a fearful outburst from someone else is an expression of love, either verbally spoken or quietly embraced in the mind. Countering fear with a fearful expression, which is what all anger engenders, will not result in a peaceful moment in the life of anyone. Giving peace a chance by remaining quiet is a gift to all of us.

✦

Being quiet in the face of a potential disagreement is actually quite rewarding because of the relief it offers. We don't have to engage in any negative dispute. We don't have to engage in any conversation of any kind, in fact. Let's consider standing aside today.

DETACHMENT IS FAR MORE ANALOGOUS TO UNCONDITIONAL love than to acquiescence. It means letting our loved ones make their own choices, and that doesn't mean we don't care. On the contrary, we care so much about them that we know they must travel their own path, rather than ours. Detachment might well be considered one of the most loving of all responses to those who travel with us. While it's true, as I have written elsewhere, that we travel intentionally with specific people, we do it in concert as learning partners, not as mirrors of one another.

Detachment is a gift to each of us, really. Whether we are detaching from others or they from us, it's a show of respect every time. To not allow others, or to not be allowed, to make personal choices limits our growth. Our time *here* is purposeful. If we steer others in a direction that's not right for them now, time is wasted, lessons are postponed, and opportunities are missed. They will come again, of course, but not letting them pass us by the first time they visit does mean we are certain to fulfill our purpose in a timely fashion.

✦

Part of our purpose is to care. It's not to do for others what they should do for themselves, however. There is a time for helping one another and a time for detaching. Let's not confuse them.

# pause *and* reflect

Keeping life simple is one of the hallmarks of detachment.
A sense of empowerment is a guarantee when we detach.

How would you describe the simplicity you feel when you detach? If possible, share your observations with a sponsor or a friend, or write them down for your own review later.

Did you ever expect to get free of your obsession with another? How does your freedom feel?

Practice is always necessary. Are you willing? Perhaps you can create a mantra for yourself or use one of the principles from this book as a mantra. Write it down now in a journal or on a slip of paper you will leave at your desk or by your bedside.

Remember, we are not seeking perfection, but simply progress.

DETACHMENT IS A LOVING ACT AND QUITE OFTEN A VERY
difficult one. Usually we have to consciously make the decision to let someone else chart their own course and thus define
their own life. We mistakenly think that since we are traveling
together, we should be able to influence the direction a friend
or lover takes, but that's not the case. Possibly, our opinion will
be sought, and in some cases adhered to, but there are no guar-
antees. We travel side by side because of the lessons we share,
and one of the lessons we all have to learn, it seems, is that we
cannot control the actions, the opinions, or the decisions anyone
else makes.

Initially, this seems like a bitter pill to swallow. Our security
feels tied to the choices our loved ones make. Are they going
to leave us out of their plans, abandon us perhaps? As we grow
in wisdom, however, we realize how very fortunate we are that
what others do is not up to us, nor does it define us. Living
one life, *ours,* is enough to handle. Only after experiencing the
freedom of letting others be free can we truly understand the
gift of detachment.

◆

To be disengaged from what others are choosing to do will
give me extra time to do what I need to do today. That's the
primary lesson I am here to learn. I know it and believe it. I
will practice it today.

## Detachment means not letting the behavior of others cause you to suffer.

FOR PROBABLY THE FIRST FORTY YEARS OF MY LIFE, I LET what others said or did control how I felt. If they smiled, I felt appreciated and worthy. If they frowned or ignored me or spoke harshly, I felt worthless and feared abandonment. How pathetic, really. I actually didn't know there was any other way to respond to the people or the situations in my life. They defined me, with my permission. I was their victim, but I had volunteered for the position. But then in 1974, I was introduced to Al-Anon, and that's where my life began to change.

Certainly not every one needs Al-Anon to grasp the wisdom that I have come to appreciate in the rooms of recovery. But it is where I learned that the behavior of others has nothing to do with me. It defines them. It reveals how they feel about themselves. When others are not kind, it's because they are suffering in some way. I have also learned that the best response for me to make to unkind people is to silently bless them and to offer them the hand of kindness. When this is my response, then both of us feel better. Two people can get relief from suffering when one person is kind.

✦

Suffering is always optional. This is a wonderful bit of wisdom to cherish on a daily basis.

34

Detachment can be triggered by
the reminder, "Don't go there."

23

WE HOLD IN OUR MINDS WHATEVER THOUGHT WE CHOOSE.
Some of the thoughts we nurture are loving. Some are confused
and negative. Many, unfortunately, are angry and blaming. Holding resentments against others for past hurts (and that's what all
resentments are about) holds us hostage and prevents us from
experiencing the next lesson on our "list," a lesson we have been
prepared for. The simple suggestion "don't go there" can change
how we see everything about the incident in front of us. Of
course, that means it can change everything about the rest of
the day too.

We don't see things as *they* are, we see as *we* are. This is a terribly important distinction. It means that what we are judging
in others or allowing to be diminished in us is a figment of our
imagination. "Out there" matches our "in here." When we can
thoroughly grasp this realization, our life will begin to look different. The next step is that we will experience it differently too.
The learning curve is long and sometimes steep but not beyond
our capabilities.

✦

Making "don't go there" a mantra that we turn to throughout
the day can change how we experience every situation that
we don't like. It promises empowerment and peace of mind.
We deserve to make it our most useful tool.

## Detachment is not letting someone else's past determine your present.

PAST BAGGAGE SO READILY COMPLICATES PRESENT EXPERI= ences, either yours or someone else's. Accepting that the past has served whatever purpose it had and moving on is one of the primary lessons we are all here to learn. There is only *now*. Get= ting our minds around that concept truly releases us to feel the joy that awaits us in each moment. God is here, now. God was in the past too when the past was *now*. And God will be present in the future when it arrives, but we can only live one moment at a time. We will grow in gratitude for this awareness when it has fully set in.

Not giving up the past means we are chained to a time and a place that simply have nothing else to teach us. Being held hostage to anyone's past prevents us from offering to our fellow travelers what they have joined us to learn today. There will be another opportunity, of course. Our lessons follow us, and we them, until we each have fulfilled our part of the bargain. De= taining the process impedes all of us, both those dancing with us now and those dancing elsewhere. We are connected, one and all, in this circle of learning.

◆

The past controls the minds of many. But we can walk away from it, our own or someone else's past. Detaching in this way is necessary if we want to experience peace.

FOR SOME, HAVING A "LITTLE WILLINGNESS" TO SURRENDER
may sound like an oxymoron. Isn't surrendering giving up, and
isn't that an all-or-nothing act? One could say yes, surrendering
is all or nothing. But first having a little willingness might be
necessary. And this implies that if we open the door just a tiny
bit to the idea, God will help us take it the rest of the way. Surrendering with no help from our Higher Power is not easy for
most of us. We may have every intention of surrendering, and we
might manage to begin the process, but the full follow-through
is a bigger step.

The gifts we receive from surrendering are many. It's not a
defeat, ever, to surrender an argument, to detach from the struggle or the stranglehold another person has on us. Detachment
can mean something as simple as walking away from a discussion
that has no solution or excusing ourselves from an argument
that is getting out of control. Detachment doesn't mean we can
no longer love the person we may have to walk away from. It
simply means that nothing good is coming of the discussion
we are having right now, and rather than escalate it, we want
to do only what would please God. Being quiet is seldom the
wrong choice.

✦

Being willing to walk away from a power struggle (or worse)
is one of the most peaceful actions we can ever take. Doing
it without the help of God is difficult for most of us, but
seeing it as an opportunity to get closer to God makes it
more appealing and far easier.

## Detachment is noticing people without judgment.

JUDGING OTHERS IS A MAJOR ISSUE FOR SOME OF US. I AM a long way from being the woman I really want to be when it comes to this characteristic. I know that the way through this is to remember and then practice, as often as possible, thinking only those thoughts that God would want me to think. Practice doesn't make perfect, and I frequently fall far short of my goal. But asking my Higher Power to help me be loving and kind is the first necessary step to doing it.

Willingness coupled with intention, followed next by action, is what allows us to be the people we really want to be. If I don't want to let judgment rule my thoughts, I have a blueprint for making different choices. It's very freeing to walk away from judgment. It's a characteristic that cripples us right along with crippling our relationships with others. We can walk tall. We can free others and ourselves with one decision.

◆

Looking lovingly on others gives both us and them joy. Why wouldn't we want to do this?

LIVING CHAOTIC LIVES CAN BECOME HABIT-FORMING, so much so that a person doesn't even realize there is another way to exist. Some people equate chaos with excitement, in fact. And who doesn't enjoy excitement, at least occasionally? But not knowing the difference between chaos and excitement means one will likely miss the myriad opportunities to be present in the "right" way to the moment that has called. Chaos is seductive, to be sure. But so is the experience of a peaceful present once it has been cultivated.

Becoming willing to live one's experiences differently is the first necessary step to discovering the freedom promised by detaching from upheavals in the lives of others. Just because we are on the journey with someone else doesn't mean we have to respond to *their* experiences on *their* path. On the contrary, we may be traveling with them so we can show them that there is another way to see and live through a particular experience. We can never know for sure what we have been called to do. But we can know for certain that if we show up lovingly, we will be on the right track.

✦

Every day offers so many opportunities to experience chaos, but for every one of them we can make the choice to be peaceful in that moment instead.

## Detachment is "moving away" from a conversation that begins to irritate.

I SPENT YEARS OF MY LIFE THINKING I HAD TO FINISH reading every book I started. Even if I only skimmed the chapters in the middle, I needed to get to the last page. I approached conversations with others in the same stuck way. I stayed in them even when I was agitated, obviously unheard, treated disrespectfully, or worse. Learning, as I have, that I can quit a book that doesn't hold my interest or a conversation that isn't respectful of my position is very empowering. Making choices that honor us takes practice. For some of us, discovering what honors us even takes time.

Taking baby steps with this idea of detachment is a good beginning. Most of us don't come by this trait naturally. We easily get drawn into the dramas around us, particularly those involving our loved ones. It's generally with those who are the closest to us that we have the conversations that might turn tense. The good news about this is that we have daily opportunities to practice detaching our emotions from these difficult conversations. And this doesn't mean we always have to walk away. We *will learn* that we can stay in a conversation while remaining detached. That's one of the lessons we have been promised.

✦

Detachment is an exciting journey. Enjoying the fruits thereof is one of the gifts of this life.

Detachment is knowing that the mind can change if what you say to the mind changes.

29

WE SIMPLY ARE NOT ABLE TO HOLD MORE THAN ONE thought in our minds at a time. Whatever thought we harbor has been cultivated by none other than ourselves. That's both the good and the bad news of our lives. No one has power over how we think. Of course, that also means we can blame no one else for what we think! If we put good thoughts in our minds, we will express good thoughts to others. The reverse is just as powerfully true.

Being consumed with the actions of others, which can so easily happen to any of us, offers an excellent opportunity to take charge of our thinking. Letting someone else be the center of our mind, and thus of our life, means we don't have a moment's peace. It also means our own life is passing us by. It's up to us to decide what we say to ourselves. It's up to us to determine how we relate to every moment. It's up to us to change our minds so that our lives can be different. It's a simple equation: what we think is what we experience. If we want something different, only we can make that happen. Today can be the day to begin.

✦

Detachment doesn't mean not caring. It doesn't mean ignoring someone, either. It means not letting our minds be controlled by the presence of others. That's all.

LETTING THOSE WHO JOURNEY WITH US MAKE THEIR OWN
decisions is one of our most difficult lessons, I think. We too eas=
ily mistake our "being together" as the invitation to get overly
involved in one another's life. Journeying together is not about
crossing over into one another's space. In fact, it's far more likely
that it's about the exact opposite—about learning *to walk together*
but not on top of each other.

We can all remember times in our own past when someone
else insisted that we handle a situation their way. Or we can
remember from our childhood how it felt when we were rep=
rimanded for trying to do something in our own way. Being
trusted with making the decisions that directly determine the
next steps of our life is a gift we all deserve to experience. Taking
that opportunity away from others, even when we think we are
doing right by them, isn't the assignment that God has called us
to do. Giving the decision to whomever it belongs to is freedom.
We will only understand this when we practice it.

◆

Perhaps we long to make decisions for everyone we love.
But doing so is not the expression of love that our loved
ones need. They need to be trusted to make their own
decisions. Today is a good day to begin the process of trust.

# pause *and* reflect

Choice is a wonderful thing.
Choosing wisely is even better.
A wise choice, often, is to do nothing.

Today might be a great day to practice not responding, not doing anything, when the inclination to get involved first presents itself.

To step away from a situation affecting a loved one is one of the hardest things we might ever choose to do. But it will likely be the right choice to make.

Be courageous. The willingness to make the right choice is generally no more than a prayer away.

Take some time to journal about what's in your mind right now.

## 31

Detachment is "keeping it simple"—
staying out of situations that
don't directly involve you.

I USED TO THINK THE SLOGAN "KEEP IT SIMPLE" WAS LUDI-
crous. I was a complicated woman, after all, with a very responsible job, a graduate degree, and a plan for my life that didn't
leave a lot of room for either error or slacking off. And I had a
lot of people in my life that I was keeping track of. I thought
keeping it simple was denying the realities of my very busy life.
How wrong I was—and how glad I am that I was wrong.

Keeping it simple can actually mean many things, depending
on the interpreter. But one of the most powerful interpreta-
tions for me has been to walk away from situations *and people*
that don't directly involve me. My life is quite busy enough as
it is. Freeing ourselves from the seduction of getting into other
people's business isn't easy at first, not if we have had an obsession with doing that. But it can be done. Millions have done it.
We can now be an example for others, too.

◆

Minding my own business is a challenge and is exhilarating
at the same time. It can become the best of all habits to
form, one that will give me both more time
and more friends.

## Detachment is having your life be about you, not about other people.

BEING REALLY CLOSE TO ANOTHER PERSON, WHETHER IT'S a parent, a significant other, a friend, a sibling, or one of our children, feels so natural, doesn't it? We want to be close to those we love. We want to help each other make decisions, do chores, plan for the future. Walking the path with someone who is in our life is the most natural of all actions. But walking beside someone, offering an opinion when asked for it, and being supportive when it's truly an act of love is not the same as taking someone else's "work" away from them. We all have specific "assignments" in this life. Not being allowed to do our own work prevents us from realizing the growth we are here to achieve.

When any one of us fails to fulfill that which we are here to do, many others will not get the opportunity to do what they are here to do either. We are like puzzle pieces comprising a panoramic scene. Not filling in the space that's been designated as ours means the picture isn't complete. Our own life must be attended to if we are to be, *and to give,* all that we can to the circle of associates who are obviously part of our journey. Nothing is happening by chance. Those who are next to us on the path need our input perhaps, but little more.

✦

The thrill of living our lives in concert with others is great indeed. But we must have the freedom to fulfill our part of the journey alone.

## Detachment is living in our adult observer role.

BEING A SILENT OBSERVER IS AN UNFAMILIAR ROLE FOR many of us. We too often assume that our input is desired, at times even required, only because we are present to a situation. Being told that our opinion isn't necessary or even wanted can be interpreted as an affront. But we can choose to see this a different way: we can decide to enjoy the freedom this offers us. Not having to respond to the many experiences that we share with others is rather refreshing. It's good for us and for our companions, too.

The idea of detachment doesn't mean we don't care what's happening to others. Nor does it mean that what's happening has no effect on us. It simply means that we don't have to react to any situation. We can observe it, make a judgment about it, and then choose a proper response if one is actually called for, or perhaps not respond at all. Practicing not responding is highly recommended if we want to grow in an important way. Making no response will become easier in time, and it sets a wonderful example for others, too.

◆

Observing what's going on around us without comment takes willingness and, on occasion, great strength, too. But detaching from others so they can do their own work is part of our work, too.

Detachment is not being dependent
on others for good feelings.

34

REACHING A STATE OF WELL-BEING THAT ISN'T RELIANT
on anyone else's actions is what we all hope for and what most
of us strive for. Celebrating our worthiness, regardless of how
others might be responding to us, isn't a natural act. We seem to
be far too dependent on others telling us that we are okay, either
through words or deeds. The joy of experiencing a moment,
now and then, when we simply know we are fine regardless of
what others are doing or saying is so much appreciated.

Being detached doesn't mean we are oblivious to the
thoughts, feelings, or actions of others. It just means that how
we feel about ourselves isn't controlled or even compromised
by what others are doing. We are on parallel journeys, complementing one another but not determining the outcome for one
another. Knowing that we don't need someone else's approval
for us to do what feels right gives us the freedom and the permission to move forward in the ways we must if we are to fulfill
our purpose here.

◆

Detachment is the hallmark of a life being well lived. As
long as we rely on anyone else for our good feelings, we
can't count on ever being wholly peaceful. And that's no
way to live.

NOT BLAMING OTHERS FOR ANYTHING THAT HAS HAPPENED to us in this life is the mark of spiritual maturity. It's also a goal that most of us have to spend years striving to attain. It's not unusual to want to make others responsible for our failures or for our insufficiencies. Being told that the circumstances of our birth, the unloving parent or spouse, or the inability to master the educational system can't be blamed aren't easy pills for us to swallow. But until we say to ourselves and others, "I am wholly responsible for all that has occurred in my life," we will not be able to move out of the prison we have built for ourselves.

Being fully responsible may feel daunting initially. But taking the responsibility in small bites makes it more digestible. Believing that we did the best we could with what was available is a good place to begin. This is also a good place to begin when we think of the supposed failings of our parents. They too did the best they could. Until we can come to terms with that, most of us won't be very willing to take responsibility for what later followed in our own lives. A great analogy is to think of ourselves as toddlers trying to learn how to walk: we fall a lot. And that's okay. Getting up again is what's important.

✦

Not looking to someone else to pick us up is the mark of maturity. We are on the path of emotional and spiritual maturity right now. Moving forward a step at a time is all that's suggested.

SOME SAY THERE ARE NO VICTIMS, ONLY VOLUNTEERS.
When I first heard that phrase, I was mystified. How could a
person who suffered at the hands of another be considered a
volunteer? But volunteers we are. Lest you misunderstand, I
don't want to suggest that there are no culprits in this world. But
how we perceive those people who mistreat us is our choice. We
can see those who are mean-spirited or worse as fearful, angry
people who are looking for acceptance, even love, in the only
way they know how. We don't have to stay in their presence.
Nor do we have to approve of their actions. But we can seek to
understand them and move on.

We are moving along this path to master the lessons we have
come here to learn, and those who travel with us, our compa-
triots as well as our adversaries, are fulfilling their designated
roles too. That's not easy to fathom if what we experience is
unpleasant, but each of us is playing a part in the drama. To not
take the actions of others as intentionally hurtful is the best of
all lessons. Detaching from what we are experiencing is a possibility. Always.

✦

What a glorious day today can be if I can remember that my
experiences are part of my necessary learning curve.

Detachment is living one's own life while
letting friends and family live as they choose.

LETTING OTHERS LIVE AS THEY CHOOSE DOESN'T SOUND
that difficult, does it? At first glance, we'd probably say no, I can
do that; what do I care what others are doing? But the fact of the
matter is that most of us try, sometimes not very subtly, to control the actions of others. We too easily think we have a better
idea about how to solve a problem. Or that we know what the
preferred outcome should be. What we have forgotten, perhaps,
is that everyone has his or her own specific agenda that has been
given by one's Higher Power. When we interfere, we prevent the
growth that's intended for our companions.

The more important reason for letting go of the lives of our
companions is that we can't do what we are here to do when we
are overly focused on someone else's journey. We *travel together*.
And for that we can be very grateful. But we are running on
parallel courses. What any one of us has as a plan for the day, the
week, or one's entire life may well be affected by that which
a friend or family member is doing. But we must forge ahead
regardless and let our companions complete their journeys, too.

◆

Being on parallel courses gives each one of us courage and
strength. But not having to carry one another is the best of
all blessings.

## Detachment is never letting someone else control how we think, feel, or behave.

38

ALTHOUGH I HAVE ALREADY MENTIONED THIS EARLIER, it's worth repeating: until I read John Powell's little book *Why Am I Afraid to Tell You Who I Am?* in 1971, I had no idea how controlled I was by the very presence of others in my life, not only people I knew well but also complete strangers. If someone looked at me unfavorably or failed to look at me at all, I was consumed with doubt. Unless I was receiving nearly constant, positive attention, I felt invisible and unappreciated, certainly unloved. Being the center of everyone else's life was what my ego demanded. But it never truly happened, fortunately.

When we are the center of anyone else's life (and only someone who is very insecure would want to control us in this way), it restricts our every movement. We don't have a life of our own when we have abdicated responsibility for ourselves, all our dreams and aspirations, all our decisions and actions, to others. It's crucial that we savor the awareness that what we are here to do complements what others are here to do, too. But none of us are here to do for others what they need to be doing for themselves. This can't be overstated. Being detached, being in charge solely of one's self, is life's assignment.

✦

It's not always easy to turn away from the demands or cajoling of others. But what we may need to do is our decision, in the final analysis. Let's stick with that.

**Detachment is letting go of fear over others' behavior.**

THROUGHOUT MY OWN LIFE THERE WERE SO MANY WAYS to feel fear about what others were doing. Growing up, I was afraid of potential violence in my home. I was afraid of my dad's anger. I was afraid my best friends were going to reject me every time a new student moved to our school. I was afraid of not being picked to play kickball after school. I was afraid I would remain uninvited to a birthday party. Then when boys entered the picture, I was certain no one would want me as a girlfriend or, later, as a wife.

This overwhelming sense of fear shadowed me throughout the first three decades of my life. Until I was introduced to the concept that I had a Higher Power who traveled with me and who always "picked me" as worthy, I fought the urge to hang on to whoever wandered close by. Hanging on to others, in the way I did, suffocated many potential friendships. I really never believed it was possible to be free of the fear that crippled me. But I am. No longer do I look to others for my self-worth. No longer am I afraid. Period. What changed? I developed the willingness to believe that life gives us the journey we were meant to have and that we aren't alone on this trip. And this willingness is available to all of us.

✦

What anyone else is doing doesn't determine who we are or what we are worth. That's an awareness that makes all the difference in the world to people who doubt.

Detachment is freedom from relying
on others to complete our lives.

40

HAVING OTHERS IN OUR LIVES TO COMPLEMENT OUR journey is a gift we all deserve. But being dependent on their presence in order to feel secure is not healthy. Nor is being so independent that we want no one else to share our path with us. Being interdependent is the best of all possible choices.

Joining with others, wherever they are, is an easy way to make a contribution toward the peace that's so often missing in families and communities everywhere. But joining with someone is not the same as denying who we are in order to fit in or to be valued. Joining with another is about giving up the idea that we should compare ourselves or compete with each other. It's about saying, "We are one"—interconnected, rather than separate. It's an act of love. It's not possession. When we join, everyone remains free. And valued. We simply don't have to share every opinion.

◆

Our lives are complemented by others but not completed by them. For this we can be very thankful. It allows us to be who we are meant to be.

# pause *and* reflect

Let the chaos that others create be theirs to resolve.
It's okay to leave a room or a conversation if the tension
   is rising.
Let's not let anyone else determine how we feel.
The past is gone. Don't try to resurrect it.

Opening our minds to a new way of seeing takes a willingness that isn't always easy to muster, but it will come. What have your attempts at this taught you?

Keep a tally for a few days of all the times you walked away from a potential argument. How does detaching from others make you feel? Find someone to share your thoughts with or write them down in your journal.

TO BE PEACEFUL MEANS NOT LETTING ANYONE ELSE'S behavior control how we feel about them, about ourselves, about the moment, or about the situation at hand. In other words, being totally free of any external influence is the only thing that can guarantee sustainable peace. We do have that option; we seldom exercise it, however. Far more often we let the mood swings or actions of others determine our own moods and behaviors. What a refreshing idea to know that we have *made* that choice. It's not required! We can make another choice.

Detachment, fully expressed, may seem a bit extreme. But like the ever-so-common phrase "You can't be a little bit pregnant," you can't be a little bit detached. We are either our own person or we are not. To be fully detached doesn't mean ignoring the others on our path, nor does it mean being unkind. But it does mean we make our own decisions regardless of the opinions and plans of others. Peace is the gift that's realized when we decide who we will be and then be it.

✦

Isn't peace what we all want? There is a guaranteed way to get it: detach. When others are in our circle, we make sure that we stay within our own choices. We do it lovingly so all will benefit.

## 42 Detachment is a gift that we receive from our relationships well lived.

HAVING RELATIONSHIPS DOESN'T ALWAYS ENSURE THAT we enjoy them. Many of us have experienced relationships that were ill-conceived from the start. Sometimes we got into a relationship simply because it was convenient or, as in my case, because it seemed better than being alone. But relationships that aren't based on mutual values or on the willingness to respect our differences aren't destined to fulfill our yearnings, not for long anyway.

There's another element that contributes to a healthy relationship, and it's crucial if the relationship is to thrive. It's the freedom to be who we really are and allow our partner the same freedom. A healthy relationship is the sum of more than the two parts. This is where the concept of detachment enters. Not being afraid to let our relationship partner live his or her life, trusting that their choices don't have to mimic ours for us to be compatible, is a sign of strength and health. It's also the necessary sign that we are trusting our Higher Power to be in charge of the journey we each need to make.

◆

Our Higher Power never detaches from us. That's the spiritual axiom that allows us to detach from all others with the faith that whomever we need to journey with will come to us.

Detachment from others is necessary
to fully enjoy attachment to God.

43

IF OUR FOCUS IS OBSESSIVELY ON SOMEONE ELSE, WE SIM-
ply cannot be present to the people and the lessons with them
that God has planned for us. Our journey is quite intentional.
And pay attention we must. Actually, that's a relief, isn't it? It
means we don't have to let the actions of others take over our
minds. We don't have to let their opinions, their outbursts, their
sulking, or their silence define us in any way. *Letting them be* gives
us the opportunity we need to connect to our Higher Power
with the fullness of our hearts. Learning to journey *with others* is
the paramount lesson for many of us.

In our attachment to God we are helped to clearly understand the work we have been born to fulfill. Each one of us is
unique and able to perform our specific tasks as no one else can.
And in order for every task to be completed, it takes every one
of us to do our part. We can be supportive of one another. We
should be, in fact. But we must let the completion of the details
be handled by the person assigned to them.

✦

There is such joy in feeling attached to God. It means
there is no fear. We will not doubt our worth. We will know
that we have a purpose, and we will know how to fulfill it
because God will supply all the information we need.

## Detachment is knowing that others' criticisms are about them.

I GREW UP IN A HOUSEHOLD WHERE CRITICISM WAS COM-
mon, far more common than praise, in fact. I don't think it was
that my parents didn't love me or my siblings, but rather, they
didn't feel satisfied with themselves, and that made it quite difficult to be satisfied with anyone else, either. So I think their
being critical of others became a habit. I observed them being
critical of their siblings, as well as of their neighbors. In fact, they
seldom praised others at all.

I look back on those years with an understanding that I
wasn't capable of then. And a sadness that my parents didn't feel
okay about who they were, which in turn made them unable to
see the good in others.

People who truly know God don't criticize. Even when they
observe a behavior that concerns them, they are far more likely
to say a silent prayer. They seem to instinctively know that their
purpose in another's life is to offer love and support, and forgiveness, should that be called for. We are never called to be
critics of one another. Way-showers, yes, but never critics.

◆

Being criticized by others need not affect how we feel about
ourselves. And it won't the more we practice detachment.

ATTACHING OURSELVES TO ANYONE BUT OUR HIGHER
Power makes us unduly influenced by the mood swings, the
opinions, the behaviors, and the judgments of whoever is on our
path. When we live that way, we have no life of our own. On
the other hand, being "attached" to God means we will be given
constant direction and feedback for the decisions we are making. Being connected to our Higher Power in this way doesn't
restrict our movements. In fact, we can ignore the directions we
get. But the good news about being attached to God is that we
will never be misled. And we will experience greater peace on
our journey.

Attaching to others, rather than to God, will never sustain us
in a healthy, peaceful way. In fact, we may feel as though we're
on a roller coaster. Allowing someone else to control us by their
mood swings becomes a habit and destroys our self-esteem. We
give our power away by choice. It's never demanded of us, and
it's never, ever a good choice.

◆

> Being connected to others is a natural desire. But there's
> a healthy connection and then there's an unhealthy
> attachment. Do we know the difference?

## Attachment to anyone other than God imprisons us.

FOR THE FIRST THREE DECADES OF MY LIFE, I REVELED IN being "necessary," or so I thought, to someone else's life. If that someone was happy, so was I. If they were sad, I tried to make them feel better. If they were angry, I was certain I had done something wrong. My every mood was controlled by the feedback I received, either verbal or nonverbal, from them. My growth was stunted, and I didn't even know it.

It wasn't until I got involved in Twelve Step recovery that I discovered there were other ways to experience one's life. Coming to appreciate that we are on shared journeys, not the same journey, has taught me many things. I have learned that what someone else sees is not what I need to see, that what they think need not be what I think. That how anyone else behaves doesn't have to chart my course too. We are complementary to each other. We are not empowered to be in charge of one another.

◆

Being imprisoned by our attachments to the people in our lives keeps us from living the journey we are here to enjoy. It's up to us to release ourselves.

Detachment is not letting the mood swings
of others determine your own mood.

47

IN THE EARLY 1970S, I READ A PASSAGE IN A BOOK BY A
popular Jesuit priest that rocked my world. I realized then that
my life had always been a reflection of how others responded
to me. If their response was loving, I felt secure. If they seemed
distant, I felt rejected. If their interests or activities didn't include
me, I could only interpret this as abandonment. I needed to be
the center of any loved one's life, and when that wasn't the case,
which was frequent, I was an emotional basket case. My life
depended on others' inclusion of me in their every waking mo=
ment. Needless to say, I had no real life.

Letting someone else's behavior control our behavior negates
our freedom of choice. It means we fail to experience the gifts
of happiness and empowerment that come with making our
own decisions. We can't fulfill the assignment that is solely ours
if we are at the mercy of someone else's behavior, even part of
the time. And if we aren't doing that which we were born to
do, we also slow down the progress of those who travel with us.

*

We are part of an orchestra, you and I. We each have a
song, a tune, to play. Yours isn't mine, and vice versa. Being
in charge of our own notes is the ultimate lesson for each
one of us.

## 48 Detachment is practicing the awareness that changing our thoughts can produce changed feelings.

WE CAN CHANGE OUR MINDS, AND THE EXPERIENCES IN our life will reflect the change. For instance, try this experiment. The next time you are impatiently standing in line at the grocery store, say to yourself, "Everyone in front of me is here by divine appointment and needs my blessing." Then notice how differently you feel inside. Notice how others begin to soften their gaze, too. If you see no change the first time you try this, try it again. It works. When we change how we see others in our world, they do seem to change as well. They will begin to match our picture of them.

Coming to appreciate that we are not powerless over what we nurture in our minds, that we are, in fact, in charge of our thoughts, gives us the hope and the promise that we can feel however we want to feel. We can be as happy, as hopeful, or as miserable as we want to be. No thought can hold us hostage. No feeling can hold us hostage. No person can hold us hostage. We are as free as we want to be. This gives us all the ammunition we will ever need to know that all is well. Always, all is well.

✦

Thoughts and feelings are intertwined. The good news is that each one of us is in charge of how we feel because of what we think. Our present is up to us.

Detachment is knowing that happiness
is the by-product of how we live our
lives, not how others are living theirs.

49

ALLOWING OTHERS TO BE GLAD OR SAD, AND KNOWING IT
doesn't relate to us, is real freedom. But coming to understand
this way of life takes time, a willingness to believe in this as a possibility, and then perseverance. Few develop this awareness instantaneously. But whenever we accept this as a path for living, it
becomes the first day of real freedom that we'll ever experience.

Tying our happiness to anyone else means we probably also
tie our sadness or confusion or depression to them, too. And
many of us do live this way, or did. I have to admit this was my
path for many years. Whatever anyone else said or did, however
anyone else felt, was what determined my emotions. It's a bit
embarrassing to say that I lived this way into my late thirties.
And if I had not been introduced to a Twelve Step program
then, I might still be tying my star to someone else's dream. Or
nightmare. My path was not unusual. I know many others who
struggled with the same issue; some still do. Our culture encourages it. But we can live differently. I know, because I do now.

◆

Happiness, as Abe Lincoln said, comes when we make up
our minds to be happy. What freedom and joy this ensures.
It allows us to model happiness for others, too.

**Detachment is not needing attention from others to feel okay.**

It's a common desire, for many of us, to want others to notice us, particularly when we are in the spotlight for a particular reason. Being listened to at home and by friends is important too. But that's not the crux of this principle. It's about getting comfortable enough with who we are to feel okay wherever we are, with or without the attention of others. Up to a certain age, many children seem to naturally have this confidence. And then they often lose it; some never regain it. But those who seek to understand themselves as well as others can generally reclaim it in time.

Not *needing* attention from others is far different than not *wanting* someone's attention. Being dependent on getting someone's attention holds us hostage to every relationship and situation we find ourselves in. It doesn't allow us to work in equal partnership with others. It doesn't free us to be who we are in the moment. We will be on guard to be who we think we need to be in order to stay in the good graces of our "captor." We are not really living when that's our path.

✦

Checking our motives for our actions is very important. Are we doing what is in our hearts? Or are we doing what we think we need to do in order to get positive attention from others?

# pause *and* reflect

God is the only partner we need to complete our life.
Attachment to God is good; attachment to others is bad.
When others criticize us, remember, it's really about them.
Our happiness reflects how we are living, not how others
   are living.
Changing a thought about anyone or any situation might be
   the first step to changing the rest of our life.

It's not rocket science to create a more peaceful life. Begin by minding your own business. Practice this as many times as you can today. Share the results with someone.

Make a small chart of those thoughts you truly want to change. Then check them off each time you succeed.

Detachment is being able to care deeply
about a situation or another person
from an objective point of view.

THERE IS A DIFFERENCE, A RATHER SIGNIFICANT ONE,
between caring for someone or some situation subjectively as
opposed to objectively. From a subjective point of view, we are
overly involved or influenced by someone's personality, perhaps,
or by their response to us. Or maybe it's a cause that has caught
our attention to the point of obsession. Not letting our emotions get out of balance for any reason allows us to offer what
we really need to in every experience that touches us.

Being objective doesn't mean we don't care. On the contrary, it means that we will likely care, *or not,* for the correct,
perhaps more rational, reasons. It often means our response can
be trusted to have been freely offered, not coerced. It means we
aren't being unduly pressured to be for or against a person, an
opinion, or a situation. Being able to stay detached when much
of the world is trying to claim our adherence to a particular
perspective is freedom at its best.

✦

Not being unduly influenced to be for or against a person or
a situation gives us the breathing room we need to make up
our own minds. Detachment, in this regard, lets us change
an opinion at our own pace.

Detachment is not creating or preventing a crisis when it's clearly not our business to be involved.

STEPPING AWAY FROM A SITUATION OR ANOTHER PERSON'S experiences when we aren't directly involved may seem unkind initially, especially if the person involved is a loved one. But whatever is happening in his or her life is for them to sort out, not us. Perhaps it's acceptable to offer a suggestion, *if asked,* but if we get involved where and when we shouldn't, we will short-circuit the journey that needs to be made by them.

There's an occasional situation in which a child is faced with a dilemma, and in that instance, we may need to be involved; but even then, we have to appreciate that the child's journey is his, not ours. We can offer guidance, and probably should, but the outcome of the situation is between him and God. We are not, in the final analysis, part of the mix. And if a crisis occurs anywhere, unless we are part of the problem, it is not ours to fix.

✦

Recognizing our limitations when it comes to the experiences of others can be troubling initially. But we will see this as freedom if we are willing to believe that God's plan for us is to live our own life, not someone else's.

## 53 Detachment is letting others have their own opinions.

MY FAMILY OF ORIGIN DIDN'T ALLOW FOR DIFFERING opinions. My father insisted that we agree with him, or all hell broke loose. Whether the topic was politics or music, his opinion was the only right one and having one that ran counter to it was evidence of insubordination. I locked horns with him for years. I felt compelled to disagree, on my own behalf and on behalf of my mom and younger brother, too. My older sisters seldom got involved in "the dance" he and I did, a dance that continued long after I left home.

I grew into adulthood steeped in this pattern of behavior, a pattern that didn't allow much room for discussion with anyone. I had to be right, just as my dad had had to be right. It wasn't until my own recovery from drugs and alcohol that I understood what the need to be right was about. Fear was the root cause for my dad's attempts to control how others thought. Fear prompted my own, too. Now I know there is nothing to fear. We come together by design. We learn by design. We let go, we detach, by design too, and peace blossoms within.

◆

Letting go of someone else's journey is the most freeing experience we can have today. And it's by far the best gift we can offer someone, too.

Detachment is knowing that what
others do is not a reflection on you.

IT'S NOT UNCOMMON TO ASSUME THAT SINCE WE ARE
generally in the company of family and friends, that our journeys must be similar. And there always will be some aspects that
are similar. But what any one of us is here to learn is quite specific. The reason we are journeying side by side is that we need
each other for support and suggestions; there is a difference,
however, between sharing what has worked for us and trying to
control how someone else should live his or her life.

Being able to detach from our loved ones is seldom easy. It
doesn't feel natural. In fact, it more commonly feels unsympathetic and self-centered. But that's the value of practice. We
learned our math tables by practicing them. We learn how to
be skillful at golf or tennis or bridge through many hours of
practice. In fact, Malcolm Gladwell, author of *Outliers: The Story
of Success,* says that the key to success in any field requires practicing for it for ten thousand hours. Detaching is a skill too, and
we can hone it if we are willing to work at it. The payoff is that
our companions learn how to take responsibility for themselves
and then rely on their Higher Power, and we learn how to
focus on the only journey over which we have any real control:
our own.

✦

Watching our loved ones move through their experiences,
and praying for them if the need arises, is our assignment,
little else.

## Detachment is knowing that you are not God.

ERNEST KURTZ WROTE A BOOK, PUBLISHED IN 1979 AND later expanded and republished in 1991, titled *Not-God: A History of Alcoholics Anonymous.* I remember thinking it was a strange title. I didn't see how my attempts to control the outcomes in my life or the life of a loved one was playing God. I was just trying to be helpful. Admitting that I had no control was too frightening. Others might leave me if I didn't try to control their movements. My future plans might not materialize if I wasn't in control of them, or so I thought back then. Letting go of any person or situation, allowing the future to unfold as it might, was simply unfathomable.

The wisdom to let go, to detach from all behaviors or situations except those that directly involve us, exemplifies freedom. But many of us don't seek freedom. We want enmeshment. We feel more comfortable in the throes of the chaos of someone else's life. And until we have experienced freedom from this kind of attachment, and the joy it offers, we will continue to search for the person who will allow us to choose his or her life to live, rather than live our own.

◆

Giving up control may be the scariest thing we will ever do. And also the most rewarding. There is only one God, and we are not it.

Detachment is no longer succumbing
to the suggestions of others when
they are not right for us.

BEING A PEOPLE PLEASER CAN CAUSE US GRIEF IN MYRIAD areas. For one, we can find ourselves knee-deep in the affairs of others far too often by getting talked into participating in experiences that don't honestly appeal to us. We might agree to help a friend (because we feel we must) when we really don't have the time, the money, the interest, or the energy. And every time we give a little bit of ourselves away in any of these ways, we lose the freedom and the time to devote ourselves to those special tasks that have been designated as ours while here in this life.

It's not easy to say no when asked to do something. It's not easy to decline a suggestion about how to handle a problem when a friend is offering it in kindness. But we must learn to *read ourselves* and listen to our inner guide. If something doesn't feel right, it probably isn't. Others are on our path for a reason, that's true. But doing someone else's will is not why they are there. Saying no thank you may well be the biggest lesson and the most frequent opportunity we will experience every day.

✦

The times when we can say no, in a kind way, rather than saying yes and then resenting it, will occur, on a daily basis. This can make the next twenty-four hours rather interesting, too.

Detachment is being able to walk away
from situations that are not helpful to us.

I HAVE PRACTICED THIS VERY SUGGESTION TENS OF THOU-
sands of times in the last thirty years. That's why I know it's possible. I won't pretend that it was easy the first few hundred times,
however. I often had to force myself to leave a room or an argument or sometimes even a relationship. Too often I felt that just
one more word from me would convince the other person that
I was right. My inability to walk away escalated many disagree-
ments. Frankly, I don't think I even realized I had a choice to do
it differently. What glory there is in knowing that that's not the
case. And in having the willingness to practice it.

Detaching from situations that are not helpful is one way
every one of us reading this could add more free time to the
day. Detaching from situations that are not helpful is a sure way
of allowing for greater peace in our lives, too. But even more
important, every time we choose this peaceful path, we add to
the peace that's felt around the world. One peaceful act is always
multiplied many times over.

◆

Throughout the day we will confront many experiences
that are best ignored or forgiven. The question is, can we?
Every time we make the better choice for our peace of
mind, we are making it for the peace of mind of millions of
others, too.

Detachment is knowing that your life
is God's business, not yours.

58

ACCEPTING THAT MY LIFE WAS GOD'S BUSINESS—AND *NOT
my own*—initially confused me. I didn't doubt that God played a
part in my life. I believed that God had a part in everyone's life,
in fact. But I was sure that my part was bigger than God's, that
I had to create my life and that all the experiences that came
calling were because of my actions. Listening to the inner voice
and then doing the next right thing hardly seemed like a big
enough part to be playing.

Giving our Higher Power control over our lives doesn't mean
we no longer need to take responsibility for our actions. Instead,
it means that what comes our way is meant for our growth *and
has been quite specifically sent,* and that we do have a partner who
will help us make whatever decision we need to make. We are
not alone, not now or ever. God is present and is sending us the
lessons that are ours to learn in concert with the Divine plan
that includes all of us.

✦

Responding in a loving, accepting way to the experiences
that are sent to us is all that's expected of us. We don't have
to fret over anything. We need not wonder what our next
assignment should be. It will come calling.

# 59

## Detachment is knowing what is not your business.

THIS IS A SIMPLE PRINCIPLE, REALLY. WHAT IT COMES down to is this: nothing is our business that doesn't directly involve us. Our family members need to do their own "work"; our friends do, too. The strangers whose paths we cross are there intentionally, that's a given. But that doesn't mean their lives are ours to control. Our journeys are intersecting for what each one of us needs to learn, and on many occasions, the lesson is simply this: mind your own business.

Minding our own business is not an unloving act. It doesn't preclude listening to a friend. Nor does it mean we can't share our own experience, strength, and hope if asked to do so. Minding our own business frees us to live our own lives. But even more important, it frees our fellow travelers to make their own discoveries and learn how to listen to their own inner guides. Once we get the feel of minding our own business, we realize how much more peaceful life can be.

◆

If peace is what we long for, there is one sure way to get it: we mind our own business.

74

WHEN WE ARE OVERLY FOCUSED ON THE OTHER PEOPLE on our journey, even the loved ones who are with us by choice, our minds are not quiet enough to hear the guidance that our Higher Power is trying to share with us. Our journey belongs to God; it's His or Her business. We have been selected to be present in the lives of those people traveling with us, but we are not present to direct those lives. Rather, we observe those lives, sharing our experience, strength, and hope when it is requested.

Releasing others to make their own journeys is not an easy concept. Our natural inclination is to offer guidance even when it's not sought. But that prevents two key things from happening: our companion doesn't hear what they need to hear from God, nor can we hear the message our Higher Power may be trying to send to us. But we are making progress. Every day this is so. And practice coupled with willingness is all that's necessary.

✦

Being detached from the experiences, particularly the problems, of others gives us the time we need to learn all that we are here to learn. We will not feel overburdened if we remember this.

# pause and reflect

Not playing God means freedom.
Living with integrity promises living with a peaceful heart.
Knowing what is not our business is a glorious realization.
Some say there are two kinds of business: "my business" and
    "none of my business."

I have found it quite revealing and even fun to discover the times I am interfering when I need to step back. Perhaps you will want to take notice too.

Every day most of us fudge a bit when it comes to having integrity. Are you willing to own those times? Are you able to see the internal impact they have?

These ideas might all be fruitful ones to journal about. Growth is generally a by-product of journaling.

## Detachment is letting others take care of their own affairs.

IT SEEMS LIKE SUCH A SIMPLE DECISION TO LET OTHERS be in charge of their own affairs. However, we quite mindlessly put our attention on others with more than frequent regularity. Particularly among many of us who caringly raised children, we developed a habit that we transfer to other people who really don't need our care. The habit becomes ingrained, and then we find ourselves in the position of doing for others what they really must do for themselves.

I don't mean to suggest that we can't help others. Being kind and accommodating are worthy traits. But we really must establish boundaries between what is helpful and what is suffocating. No one accomplishes what they are here to learn when any one of us does too much. The real beneficiary of letting others be in charge of their own affairs is ourselves, of course. It gives us more time to grow and to play.

◆

Practicing detachment must happen before it becomes an accomplished skill. For most, it's a daily practice, in fact. And that's okay. It's worth it.

THOSE PEOPLE ON OUR JOURNEY ARE BLESSINGS, FOR SURE. Every one of them, even those who seem difficult to be around. It's been said by the really wise that the more difficult an encounter, the greater the lesson and the ultimate wisdom gained. But if we let the presence of anyone on our path, those we adore as well as those we abhor, sidetrack us from the "work" we are here to do, we will be cheating ourselves. And when we cheat ourselves, we are cheating everyone else too. That's simply how it works. Our interconnection to all humanity makes this so.

Attaching ourselves to others seems like a natural response. The feeling of aloneness, of separation from others, is palpable and haunting. So then we cling to whoever wanders too close, much like a moth to flame. This isn't something to be ashamed of, however. Wanting connection with others is good. It's normal. It's also very healing for both parties. But nurturing a connection for the purpose of healing our wounded inner spirit and forming an attachment that stifles the growth of either party are not the reasons we have found each other on this journey. We have found each other solely to act as listeners, healers, prayerful companions, not to be hostages to each other.

We are free to grow and help each other grow. Consider every expression of consideration like the raindrops that are so necessary to the seedlings a farmer plants each spring. We are doing our part every time we offer an attentive heart. Nothing more is asked of us.

◆

Being free to love and honor one another is the purpose of the journey. We can do this only when we allow our companions the freedom they need, the same freedom we too must value.

*DETACHMENT IS A COLD=SOUNDING WORD, ISN'T IT?* It suggests being unsympathetic, perhaps ignoring someone, or even worse, shunning them completely. Many are confused when they first hear the word. It wasn't until I sat through many Al-Anon meetings and read a lot of literature about letting others make their own journeys that I managed to get a glimmering of what *detachment* meant. My respect for the others on my path grew as a result of what I was learning, and this fostered greater respect for myself.

My guess is that your experiences somewhat mirror mine. Walking beside others is what we are here to do. That's why others have gathered. But walking side by side is far different than pushing our specific direction on someone else. If our motive is to express joy about another's journey, allowing her or him to have what fits for them, we are fulfilling God's will for us. If, instead, we are directing traffic, we have usurped God's role in their lives, and it's time to back off.

Recognizing when it's time to back off isn't easy. I have been *practicing* detachment for many years and I still want to be the traffic cop at times. But I have learned a valuable lesson that I'd like to share. Whenever I decide to "take over," or try to, it's because of fear, oftentimes an unnamed fear, but fear nonetheless. At these moments, taking a deep breath and seeking to feel the presence of my Higher Power allows me to shift my perspective and get into right relationship with Him.

Nothing about this is easy. But every effort we make adds peace to the world around us. And that's a worthy commitment.

✦

Deciding to walk away from a person or a situation, instead of insisting we should be in charge, is appropriate unless we are directly being affected. Being willing to honestly assess our necessity to the outcome is the key.

**Detachment can be enhanced by prayer.**

VERY FEW PEOPLE ARE BORN WITH THE NATURAL CAPACITY to detach from the struggles, the anger, or the personal failures of those they love. I believe my own fear of how others' behavior will affect me has prompted me to want to control others' actions, opinions, and even their long-term goals. Learning to live without this inclination is what the journey is about. And it's a daily reprieve when I practice letting go and relying, instead, on the Serenity Prayer when confronted with those situations and people who seem to be screaming for my involvement in their lives.

Embracing detachment is a wholesome commitment to make. It doesn't make a culprit of anyone. Nor does it hold anyone hostage to whims and opinions. And best of all, it allows us to pursue the work that's truly ours to do. Lest I make this sound too easy, let me assure you that I have spent years practicing this behavior.

At first I thought detachment meant ignoring others, turning my back on them completely. A mentor helped me to see that detachment meant loving others in the truest sense: letting them grow into their own skins, and not be extensions of me. What has made my occasional success with detachment possible, however, is vigilant prayer. God can do for us what we cannot do for ourselves.

I wish I could say that I embrace healthy detachment every day, but some days I cling, some days I manipulate. Some days I am fearful and react in ways that surprise me. But I am teachable. We all are.

✦

Being open to prayer is a way to discover the power of detachment. It strengthens our willingness to live differently; to see God as a companion, not as a stranger; and to claim Him as a solution to anything that's troubling us.

THE WORD *HOSTAGE* CARRIES WITH IT SUCH A NEGATIVE connotation, doesn't it? It brings to mind war, prison camps, abductions, and criminal activities. In this book, "hostage taking" has a less sinister meaning, but it's still insidious if allowed to fester. Taking a hostage might be little more than the focused attention we devote to others. It could mean clinging tightly to someone as they are trying to spread their wings. It may feel like love to the "host," but to the hostage it generally feels suffocating.

Before I found the recovery rooms, I was an expert at hostage taking. If we are uncertain about our own path, our own future, if our own connection to a Higher Power is not secure, we can transfer that need for security into a need for constant attention from and for another person, an activity that will cause a friendship to wither and die. Our role in one another's life is to nurture growth and peace and wholeness. This can only happen when the touch we offer one another is light, not tight. When we release rather than grasp. When we celebrate freedom, not stifle it.

It is possible to learn how to detach. As I have shared already throughout this book, I am a work in progress. What's crucial to understand is that the hostage taker is in prison right along with the hostage. No one wins. No one grows. No one walks her intended path if bound to another person. If this message speaks to you, then *let go. Now.* The time is right. For both of you.

◆

Helping each other with a concept like detachment is such a blessing. Walking the walk is the best way to help, but sharing our experience, strength, and hope is helpful too. We travel together as way-showers. Imitating unhealthy behavior is not what we are here to learn. From among those we observe, let's carefully choose the behaviors that will enhance our own and others' lives today.

Detachment is letting the outcome of
another's behavior be their problem.

LETTING A FRIEND OR FAMILY MEMBER EXPERIENCE THE
consequences of his or her actions is not an easy decision to
make. But it's the right decision. If we try to lighten their consequences or assume them ourselves, we are interfering with the
growth our companion is scheduled to experience. If we could
only think of it in that way, we'd be better able to let go. We are
*scheduled* for certain experiences as we journey along this path,
every one of us. Learning how to detach is on our schedule, or
we wouldn't be sharing this book!

Thinking of it in this way makes the practice of detachment,
which isn't all that easy, far less frustrating and more exciting.
Knowing that we are being given these opportunities and challenges because we are ready for them, have been prepared for
them in fact, and are serving as examples to others of what detachment looks like makes our work here far more meaningful.

Our purpose in life is not always clear to us. Nor does it need
to be. Likely we have more than one purpose in a lifetime. But
clearly, showing up lovingly in the lives of others is one of the
purposes we all share, and there isn't a more loving way to show
up than to act as a witness to another's growth. Being a witness
means being an observer. It doesn't mean interference. It doesn't
necessarily require any words. It may mean quiet prayer, on occasion. It may mean offering a suggestion but only if one is requested. Witnessing is simply casting a loving eye on the person
who has crossed our path for the moment or for a lifetime. This
is an assignment we can all cherish and succeed at.

◆

Being a witness to one another is a gift we can have every
moment of every day. This is why we have come together.
We are not present, in this shared space, to be in charge of
one another but to cherish the moment God has given each
of us. Relish this time of observation. And love.

Detachment is doing the "next right thing" without focusing on the outcome.

67

TURNING OVER TO GOD THE OUTCOME OF EVERY SITUA-tion allows us to act freely and with the trust that honors one's Higher Power. Our lives have been blessed repeatedly. Hindsight reveals this. Most of us can think of several times when we were "saved" from a dreaded outcome. And we know why, don't we? God had a better plan for us than the one we were crafting. Simply doing what feels right in the moment is all that's being asked of us. God is waiting to do the rest. He has always been waiting. Our job was and always will be to acknowledge Him.

This assurance is a powerful gift and one we deserve. We are God's children, after all. There was a time in my past when I recoiled at this idea. Now I am relieved by it, I am comforted by it. My problems are solved by my remembrance of it. My work is to open my heart to God's loving spirit and to pass on the peace and hope that passes through me. My job is not to direct the traffic around me. It's to witness what's present, seek a quiet place within, and ask God what my next action should be. Does that sound like a reasonable plan to you as well?

The more of us there are who step away from the role of directing the lives of others, choosing instead to pass on peace and hope and love and prayer, the greater will be the rewards reaped by all humanity. We are invited to carry this goodness forward. Letting God's will prevail in our lives and in the lives of our loved ones allows peace to prevail in our hearts; surely this is *the peace that passes all understanding.*

◆

Making our lives quieter, simpler, and more peaceful is a worthy choice. Letting God play God is how to do it.

WE CAN LIVE PARALLEL AND COMPLEMENTARY LIVES, WITH intense and intimate joining, while not stifling each other's journey. Each of us has been called to handle particular tasks, and we can appreciate those persons close at hand as witnesses. But that doesn't imply that we need their approval or involvement to fulfill our purpose. Living in community, not in isolation, is the passageway to the healing. But living *with others* does not mean *on top of* others.

How freeing it is to know that we share this journey by design. Each one of us has a Director who works in concert with us. We are the players, and the encounters we have with others happen according to the script that is destined to move us forward, says Caroline Myss, spiritual author and medical intuitive. The script does not have to be figured out alone. We have the spiritual guidance of God and angels to see us through the good times and bad. They will balance each other out, even though we may feel that the bad times are relentless. It's during those times that we may wish we could be dependent on others. It's natural to feel that way. And it's also fortunate that we are learning that healthy relationships rely on us relying on God and not on our human support system for our answers.

Being dependent on the actions of any person for our preservation or our definition has become a habit for many of us, and it prevents us from connecting with the spiritual forces that are available to us, the very forces that have been assigned to us. Our answers are waiting for us. Let's not tarry.

✦

Being too dependent on someone else for any reason doesn't allow us to fully experience the sacred moments of our lives. Let's not throw away those moments.

Detachment is showing by example,
not words, how our lives can change.

I WAS AT A GREAT AL-ANON MEETING TODAY WHERE BOTH
men and women shared how their lives had changed as the result
of practicing the principle of detachment. After years of plead=
ing, cajoling, and being angry and resentful with their "qualifier,"
they finally just accepted that their loved ones' journeys were
none of their business. The particular gift of this meeting was
that a newcomer was able to hear the wisdom from all these
people, wisdom each one had acquired over the last few months
or years of coming to the fellowship.

Because each person who shared offered examples of how
their behavior had changed, the newcomer was able to see that
she could change her behavior too. Never was it guaranteed that
the behavior of the addict would change, but the behavior of
everyone else around the addict could and will change, in fact,
if the principle of detachment is practiced.

That's the beauty of sharing our experience, strength, and
hope. Our failed past attempts to control someone on our path,
when shared with others, can serve as examples that giving up
control, as quickly as possible, will assure the best results. And
it will allow the "controller" the relief she deserves, relief that
will become inner peace in due time. Every one of us who
sits in these meetings is being schooled in a new way of seeing
and acting. An additional payoff is that the more any one of
us minds our own business, the less we are contributing to the
level of tension in our homes. The ripple effect of that decision
is phenomenal.

*

There are two kinds of business: my business and none of
my business. This is a principle that can and will change
every discussion that any one of us has. I invite you to
practice this. And then watch the miracles occur.

REMOVING OURSELVES FROM THE THICK OF A SITUATION that is really none of our business is another way of interpreting the meaning of detachment. It doesn't mean being uninterested in the people who are close to us or in the ultimate outcome of a situation that has ensnared one of them, or not caring about the well-being of anyone else. It simply means letting the affairs of others belong to those rightful parties. This is really good advice and definitely the advice we'd get from a wise grandparent or mentor or God if we sought God's help.

But thinking we need to be a critical part of the journey of every loved one, or sometimes even of mere acquaintances, and the solution that is always in process is owing to our own insecurities about letting others have their own very necessary lives, lives that may be moving in another direction without us.

Many of us have grown up in families that were overly involved in the tiny details of our lives, and our culture certainly fosters the idea that other people's business is ours to resolve. This gets played out on the international stage every day. But there is at least one other way to look at the experiences we are privy to. We can learn to believe that our best efforts on behalf of anyone, anywhere, might be a simple hope or prayer that they will be willing to listen to the interior guidance that is surely available to them. Wanting to be necessary to others is a form of codependency, and it's not in anyone's best interests. No one grows when that's the intent of our interactions.

◆

Watching the activities around us with a sense of appreciation, and the knowledge that we are being honored by the opportunity to offer our prayers on behalf of all those participants, makes our involvement what it should be: loving detachment from a distance.

# pause *and* reflect

Being a living example of detachment is being a
   great teacher.
Doing the next right thing is not a mystery. Ever.
Give up seeking to be the center of someone else's life. Now!
To stand apart from our friends does not mean we aren't
   joined in love.

Have you ever considered the role that hostage taking
is playing in your life? If not, do so now. You will recognize it by how attached you are to someone else and how
much you want their undivided attention. Consider the
down side before you lose yourself. Please journal about
this today.

## Detachment is knowing that you are not the center of anyone else's life.

SHARING OUR LIFE WITH SOMEONE CAN BE GOOD, VERY good, in fact. And intentional, an important detail of God's plan, you might even say. But living in the center of someone else's life, cut off from our own dreams and aspirations, is like being caged, and the freedom that could and should be yours to experience is missing.

We aren't present to each other here and now to act as strict bodyguards or to make demands on how life must be lived. We have divinely encountered each other because of the very special information each one of us has already acquired on our journey, information that is ready to be passed on. Giving away what we have been given is how we keep it. Remember? But if we narrow our focus too much and only dance to the tune of our current partner, we are not participating in give-and-take, and we are sidestepping what God may want next for our lives.

Living in the center of our own life may be a new experience. For all of us it's been, at some time, a learned experience that we must practice. As children we naturally gravitated to the others in our lives, letting them define us, dictate to us, control us. But we can make other choices now. And life will never look the same.

✦

Not being controlled by someone else's whims is the freedom we all deserve, but it's the freedom we may fear claiming, too. It will wait for you. And when you take the plunge, you will never look back.

MORE THAN THIRTY YEARS AGO, I READ A BOOK TITLED
*Following Your Heart's Desire.* It was an unfamiliar concept to me
then. My life had always been about trying to decipher what
was in someone else's heart and then following that intention
as though it were mine too. I truly didn't know what my own
heart desired, other than wanting to be the center of that special
person's life. I couldn't imagine even what the idea meant. Being enmeshed with the many people I journeyed with seemed
natural, as though that were our reason for being together. How
long ago that seems and how much I have learned since then!

Enmeshment is deadly, actually, because it quickly depletes
our energy. It denies the presence of the *holy voice* residing within
each one of us that desires to be heard. And it finally kills our
spirit. How sad that so many of us choose enmeshment as a way
of life anyway. Perhaps it seems easier than searching our own
hearts and minds for what matters to us. But when we don't
make the effort to discern who we need to be and what we
need to offer to those who travel with us, we are misspending
our lives and failing to reap the joys that come with following
our own hearts' desire.

Perhaps it's time to revisit how we look at the opportunities
and the people who share our current circumstances. Are we
showing up as ourselves or as caricatures that we think they
might better appreciate? If the latter, then think again. The only
time we have to be ourselves, fully, is now. That's what God
wants from us. That's what our companions prefer. And that's
what our heart desires too.

✦

Discerning where we need to be complementary and
where we need to be true to our own inner voice is a sign
of emotional maturity. It takes practice and willingness and
time. All three are available to us.

Detachment is relinquishing the role of being someone else's Higher Power.

I USED TO THINK IT WAS MY JOB TO CONTROL THE SIGNIF-icant people in my life. Having been first an elementary school teacher, where I needed to be in charge, and then the wife of an alcoholic, I easily adapted to this role, and was pretty good at it, or so I thought. But after years of frustration and deep emotional pain, coupled with a divorce and many failed relationships, I was steered to the fellowship of Al-Anon where I was told that my attempt to control others was simply never going to be success-ful. I might get acquiescence or compliance or wear someone down for a while, but actually getting them to do only what I wanted them to do would be short-lived, at best. At first, I didn't buy it. I was certain that all I had to do was figure out the right words, the right actions, the right promises, and I'd get the results I wanted. But I was wrong. Thank goodness I was wrong!

Allowing others to be responsible for themselves is like tak-ing a vacation in the middle of winter or getting a snow day when one least expects it. It's freeing. It's joyous. It releases us to explore a new activity, perhaps. And giving up trying to control others, whomever they happen to be, allows them the respect they deserve.

Our purpose in their lives may be as a way-shower, a teacher of sorts, but foisting our own way of seeing, of believing, and of acting on others isn't part of the equation that brought us together. We have come together for what we need to learn, that's true, but that doesn't include trying to take over one an-other's life.

◆

My own Higher Power is who directs my life. And you have yours too; we each have our own Higher Power. We are present to each other to be way-showers, sharing our experience, strength, and hope. And that's quite enough.

Detachment is not being diminished
by the behavior of others.

74

MY EXPERIENCE HAS BEEN THAT THIS IS ONE OF THE more difficult principles to apply. When others treat us unkindly, as they often do, it's easy to think we must have done something to deserve it. In fact, maybe we, too, had been unkind first. However, someone's actions or behavior need not determine how anyone else perceives themselves and then acts. We are "dancing" every moment with our companions, and the smoothness of the dance—or its opposite—will be felt, observed by others, and used as the stuff of interpretation for the next move. The dance, be it gentle or diminishing, will continue. Fortunately, we can decide if we want to steer the dance in a new direction.

Thinking of our experiences with others as opportunities to express *and accept* unconditional love—even when it doesn't appear to be that—is courageous, mind-altering, and wonderful preparation for every next moment in time. Deciding to believe that everyone's actions are expressing love *or a call for love* is what allows for the willingness to accept wherever someone else is on their journey. When we can nurture that, our own journey flourishes. It's not easy to say, "His actions don't determine my worth," but when we make a practice of this (and we can succeed at this task, I assure you), a path to a more loving and intimate future with all companions will become possible.

✦

The dance floor is ours and the dance is of our choosing.
Will it be a waltz, a fox-trot, or a ballet? Or will we sit on the
sidelines feeling exposed and unchosen? The choice is ours.

# 75  Detachment is keeping your feelings separate from what others are doing.

A CHILD SCREAMING ON AN AIRPLANE OR A MOTHER loudly scolding her child in a grocery store can easily stir up feelings in me. I either want to aid the child, thinking I should do something to alleviate the anguish being expressed, or I want to get out of the enclosed area immediately. In many cases that's not possible, and getting involved in the business of a parent and her child, unless the child is being injured, is never appropriate. There is a response that is, however. It's quiet but ever so effective: it's prayer. Prayer changes my inner spaces and quiets my mind and can have a positive effect anyone who might be feeling the frustration of either situation.

Detaching from the chaos of the external world, regardless of the nature of the chaos, is something I have practiced for many years. I applied this tool when mean-spirited people used to wander across my path. I find it rather interesting that since I have learned how to detach, I seldom come into contact with mean-spirited people. I think we discover in others what we expect to find. If I am expecting to be put down or ignored, just possibly that's the antenna I have extended.

In the give-and-take of our personal lives, we get what we expect, and it generally matches what we have extended. It puts the responsibility for the life we want squarely in our hands, doesn't it? But when the unexpected and frustrating do occur, we have a tool bag to use.

✦

Watching others from the sidelines is sometimes best. We need not be involved in much of what's happening in our midst. Caring about the people present is not the same as acting on their behalf. Let's make sure we know the difference.

STOMPING MY FOOT AS A KID, POUTING AND BLAMING MY brother for whatever I had been caught doing and was being reprimanded for, is a familiar memory. I hated owning up to my shortcomings. Even more, I hated the feeling that I had been caught. I still don't relish admitting my faults. Perhaps no one does. But allowing for their existence and making restitution when necessary, along with making the decision to change those behaviors that are clearly infringing on the rights of others, does free us from feelings of guilt and shame, rather than letting those characteristics define us completely.

We are never unaware of when we have harmed someone else or stepped over the line in how we responded to them, regardless of our words to the contrary. Simply feeling angry when caught or feeling unfairly treated if corrected is irresponsible and won't free us to become the persons who already are *within* us just waiting to be acknowledged.

Detachment is an interesting concept. It doesn't mean being uncaring. It doesn't mean being isolated and uninvolved. It means having emotional clarity, showing support where it's needed, making apologies where necessary, and blaming no one.

◆

Being responsible for our actions and the feelings that accompany them, and nothing more, is enough to focus on each day.

## Detachment means no longer harboring thoughts of "attachment."

OH, HOW I LONGED TO BE "ATTACHED" TO SOMEONE IN my youth, to be on his arm, so to speak! To be chosen as a girl-friend meant that I was popular, that I mattered and was truly special, at least to "him." Not being attached to someone defined me to others in a way that diminished me, I thought. It saddens me to recall how empty I felt inside back then. It was an empti-ness that I ultimately tried to fill with alcohol when having a boyfriend and then a husband didn't fill me up, but to no avail. And that's the good news, of course. It was a long journey from there to here, however, a long, sometimes very painful journey.

It wasn't until my late thirties that I began to understand how insidious my need for attachment actually was. Seeing myself only in relationship to others, always defining myself by how *I perceived* the way that others were perceiving me, meant that my very fragile persona was frequently being fractured by the whimsy of others.

It's simply not true that most people intentionally hurt us. Our collective thoughtlessness is often what is the root cause of many of the hurts we all experience. But for years I didn't know this. I assumed I deserved what *I seemed* to be getting. Know-ing this, as I now do, and having learned that others' behavior is a reflection of how they feel about themselves, has allowed me such freedom. Are you sharing in this understanding, at this stage of your life?

◆

Acting as helpmates to one another so that we all have a better understanding of what detachment versus attachment means is a great undertaking. And sharing with one another our experience is the place to begin. That's what I am trying to do here. And I hope you can see your own progress.

I HAVE A FRIEND WHOSE LITTLE BOY SEEMS UNUSUALLY able to allow other children to do whatever they are doing, even when their actions seem rude and thoughtless, without making a spiteful response. She said he doesn't come running, crying that kids are being mean. He neither hits nor yells. And he doesn't seem scared or intimidated. He simply glances at the child who is being mean and then goes on about his own business. It's as though he has an innate understanding that what others are doing doesn't have to define him, diminish him, or affect him in any way. She says she has even observed him reaching out in an inclusive, kind way to the child who has just been pushy or rude, an act that took her totally by surprise the first time she observed it.

Is Jeffrey's response to the world around him unique or were we all "Jeffreys" until we learned, perhaps at the feet of our parents, to be afraid and retaliatory? Some educators and psychologists say that most behaviors are learned. But might we possibly be born with some qualities that we unlearn as the result of the prompting we get from the adults in our lives? Children certainly observe retaliation every day, on television, in our homes, in the classroom. Might we groove a certain kind of response simply because we see it in others hundreds of times daily? Perhaps we can never know the answer to this, but we can be certain that we can change our responses, at any age, to the circumstances we find ourselves in.

◆

We can decide, once and for all, to never consider ourselves unfairly treated. What happens to us or around us is an opportunity to make an observation, say a prayer, and then move on. What freedom there is in that!

Detachment is keeping your
feelings separate from what
others are saying and doing.

THE FREEDOM TO NOT BE SHAMED, CAJOLED, OR CON-
trolled by what anyone else is doing *or saying*, is one of the gifts
I most treasure these days. I didn't know, for most of my life,
that I could live relatively unaffected by what other people were
thinking or doing. On the contrary, nearly every word spoken
or movement made by anyone within proximity to me tended
to decide my fate for that brief few minutes. Who you were and
what you said or did defined me!

The awareness that it could ever be different was a long, slow
process of learning. It only came in tiny doses, actually. I didn't
receive this gift in one "ah hah" moment. It came over time
and after listening to the wise words of many others who had
become my traveling companions on the spiritual path. How
grateful I am that we were traveling together, however, and that
I had become a willing listener.

Learning to keep our feelings separate from others does not
mean ignoring those people who walk among us. In fact, those
who walk with us are most often the teachers we have sought.
But learning from them what we need to learn does not mean
we should be treated poorly or judged in any way. Our lesson is
always meant to elevate us, to enlighten us in some way, not to
demean us in any way. And the lessons we are here to offer others follow this same pattern. It's an equal exchange of attention,
wisdom, and love. Always.

◆

Letting others be who they need to be and trusting that my
Higher Power will protect me is my best assurance of not
being controlled by the learning curve of others.

Detachment means no longer adjusting
our lives to the whims of others.

80

PEOPLE CHANGE THEIR MINDS VERY QUICKLY AND OFTEN-
times unexpectedly. That's human nature. Being able to change
when circumstances call for it is good, in fact. It means we are
paying attention to the world around us and making choices
that better fit our changing circumstances. For instance, if the
company one is working for begins to downsize, it is wise to
start looking for new work opportunities before the pink slips
are handed out.

Allowing for change, whether it is initiated by friends, by
strangers, or simply by a situation that involves us, without letting our own focus for the day be completely thrown off kilter
or undermined, is a sign of emotional maturity. This is growth
we all want to experience. The upheavals all around us, and they
are many, for sure, can be observed, learned from, incorporated
into our own way of seeing on occasion, and even *detached from*
because nothing, no one or no circumstance, has the capacity to
control our sense of self, ever.

In the early decades of my life, I constantly tried to adjust
to the whims of significant others, certain it would make me
indispensable to them. How wrong I was. We must find our
own voice and let it define us. We must find our own Higher
Power and let Him or Her guide us. We must trust that with
Spirit as the unchanging force in our life, we will always be able
to handle whatever changes present themselves. This is what has
been promised to us.

✦

Where any one of us is right now is where we can best
serve others. The changes that are manifest in anyone's life,
whether appreciated or not at the time, will become our
opportunities to rely on God to help us see our way. We can
be grateful for the whims of others when we see them from
this perspective.

# pause *and* reflect

Your life is never, ever dependent on what someone else is
doing. This is a good thing!

Letting the whims of others control you means you will live a
very uncertain, generally troubled life. Do you want that?

Being solely responsible for how you feel is an adjustment at
first, perhaps. But then it's empowering.

These ideas are new to many of us. But they are guaranteed to make life easier, more peaceful, and definitely more hopeful. But we have to stay committed to the practice that is necessary to actually change our outlook, and thus our life.

Begin the practice before even leaving your house today. Begin with asking God for help.

Detachment from others can be nurtured by strengthening our "attachment" to our personal hopes and dreams.

APPRECIATING THE DREAMS OF OUR FRIENDS CAN BE ONE of the best of exchanges between us. It thrills them to be able to share with us what excites them, and it's one of our greatest gifts to them to be a witness to the sharing of their dream and then to its unfolding. Yet, allowing *that* dream to belong solely to them and not making it our own too is very important. We each must cultivate our own dreams. That's our purpose for being here.

As with so many other lessons in my life, I had to learn this one the hard way. I didn't have my own dreams as a young woman. What my friends longed for, I wanted too. I figured this was the best way to be a stable, *unrejectable* part of the group. I carried this assumption into all my relationships throughout school and even into my first marriage. I was desperate to fit into someone else's dream. It became my dream to figure out theirs, and then adopt it too. My fear of abandonment was exhausting.

With spiritual recovery, however, came a new way of seeing the possibilities for my life, and this included the invitation to have my own hopes and dreams. Initially, I felt ill-equipped for thinking or seeing in a new way. But gradually I learned to turn to the quiet place within where I sought help. And it came. The dreams had been there all along. I took pen to paper, and the rest is history. My life became what it has become as the result of a dream and a conversation with God. I know willingness opened the door. And healthy detachment from the needs, the control, and particularly the emotions of others has become my gift. And what a gift it has been.

✦

We all have a dream waiting for us. If you have not discovered yours yet, get quiet. Close your eyes and seek to see it. It will come into view. The hovering angels are always keeping watch over our dreams for us until we are ready. This you can trust to be true.

TELLING OTHERS WHAT WE THINK IS BEST FOR THEM IS A seductive behavior that can become honed into an ingrained habit, and it's not a habit that enhances our relationships. Even when people ask us for our opinions, we need to be wary. Expressing what has worked for us, in a similar instance, is acceptable perhaps, but taking it any further than this opens us up to criticism when, and if, the suggestion we make backfires, as it most assuredly will some of the time.

According to Caroline Myss, the spiritual intuitive I earlier mentioned, we are moving through our daily lives with absolute intention and with people we have specifically selected because of our common interests and necessary lessons. We might misinterpret this to mean we are in charge of one another, but that would be wrong. Our journeys are simply complementary. As learners, we need each other, and one of our greatest lessons is the power that comes as the result of joining together, sharing our dreams, and bearing witness to one anothers' struggles and successes. Shared experiences heighten the joyous ones and lessen the painful ones. Coming together in this supportive way readies all of us for the next leg of our journeys, however they may manifest.

We are cheerleaders. We are not bosses. We are not God. We are not here to judge. We are here, sharing this space and time, as angels in disguise, making one another's journeys more peaceful.

◆

Showing excitement for each other's journey is good. But let that be enough. If something more is called for, God will take care of filling the need.

Detachment is refusing to let our
interactions with others define us.

83

THIS PRINCIPLE HAS BEEN TOUCHED ON MYRIAD TIMES
but I think it's of paramount importance, thus it bears repeating.
It is simply too easy to let the actions of others control how we
feel about ourselves. Many of us have been falling into this trap
since childhood. If they smile, I must be lovable. If they make eye
contact, I have been noticed. When they frown, I am a failure
and worthless. Examples of falling into this trap are endless.

What others do and what they say does reveal a great deal,
that's true. But what do these actions really reveal? My observations, coupled with many years of studying human behavior,
tell me that what others do and say reflects what they think of
*themselves*. In other words, when someone scolds you or me, or
attempts to, we can choose to define it as a reflection of the kind
of day that person is having. Our self-worth need not be injured
by the attack. *It's equally important, however, not to let our self-worth
be tied to the* positive *reactions of others, either.* Our self-worth is a
gift from God. Period.

Let me assure you that it's not easy to let the snarls or the criticisms or the obvious avoidance tactics of others go unnoticed.
But responding to them isn't necessary. Even though we may be
screaming inside to respond, we can let our desires slide by. We
can look on those actions quietly, noting the struggle that they
must be having, and say a quiet prayer, instead. What a change in
behavior this could be, and the real benefit is how much more
peaceful we will feel and how much more peaceful the moment
will become for all present.

✦

No one else defines us. No one. God has promised us
worthiness. And we need do nothing to deserve it or
claim it. This is a principle, a promise that bears frequent
repeating.

Detachment means no longer needing to be
in charge of anything, not even our own lives.

I HAVE HEARD IT SAID MANY TIMES IN MANY SPIRITUAL
circles that we are exactly where we need to be, doing exactly
what we need to be doing at any moment in time. This isn't an
easy principle to consistently live by, particularly if we are going
through a difficult patch of experiences. But thinking that my
plan for how my life should unfold is the right plan, the only
conceivable plan, has been proven wrong many times over the
years. Fortunately! If my plan had succeeded, on any number of
occasions, I would not be sitting here now sharing these words
with you. I'd have been buried long ago. It's as simple as that.

Allowing ourselves the luxury of becoming what God in=
tended is so much more peaceful than trying to force situations
whose time has not come. The freedom to let life simply be
whatever it will be in this moment gives us a lot of extra time
to smile at strangers, to lend a helping hand to others, to watch
children running down the street, and to appreciate the birds
chirping as we take that early morning walk.

Allowing life to *simply be* doesn't mean we stand idly by. On
the contrary, it means we honor those directions we feel God
is sending us. We listen to those words of guidance we feel are
directing our way, making sure that no matter what we do in
any given moment, we are not causing harm to someone else.
Letting go of our attachment to how our life should unfold is a
wonderful gift to give ourselves.

◆

We can trust in God's direction. Trying to be in charge of the
unfolding of our life will simply hinder the journey, throw
the outcome off course, and prevent the growth we are
ready for now.

Detachment is not disinterest, but
that might be the first step.

85

THE CONCEPT OF DETACHMENT IS GENERALLY NOT EASILY grasped. When I first heard the word, I was mystified. People told me I needed to "detach" from the troubling circumstances in my life and detach, as well, from the people I felt were causing me such grief. I wondered how I'd ever be able to change them if I detached from them. That, of course, was the whole point; we can't change others. We can't control the outcomes of the situations we are a part of. Learning how to fully detach requires a long and arduous learning curve. Staying on the learning path, regardless of how long it takes to grasp the freedom of detach= ment, becomes its own reward.

As has already been suggested, we won't learn how to detach on the first try, not even on the one=hundredth try. But we will make progress, and fleeting moments of peace will be our reward. I practiced disinterest before I was able to grasp how to detach. Detachment and disinterest are not the same, of course, but to the onlooker, the witness, they appear to be the same. I needed to act as if I were detaching even when I was still very emotionally charged up by the people or circumstances around me. I needed to prove to myself and others that I could *let them be*, that I could let be everything that involved others. And after a time, I began to like the feeling of letting go. Eventually, I cherished the moments of turning away rather than holding on to the many people I had previously sought to control.

✦

Being willing to practice baby steps of detachment is necessary. And having others witness our efforts is what keeps us on the path of this phenomenal exercise in discovering freedom.

Detachment means no longer
leading others' lives.

WALKING THROUGH LIFE WITH OTHERS IS ONE OF THE
many blessings on this journey. But we must also make our own
plans and follow our own path rather than blindly following
in the footsteps of others. Learning this can be a bit distressing,
initially. Perhaps we assumed that those who walked with us
were there on a mission and we rather liked their input. Their
presence freed us from figuring out our own lives.

But turning the reigns over to others prevents us from claiming our own opportunities. We won't become who God had
intended for us to be if we are listening to voices other than His.
When we don't know who we are, and until we have discovered our own very specific purpose here, we'll flounder and fail
to have the impact we could be having on the others we walk
among every day.

The desire to be attached to others is not unnatural. As children we attach to our mothers for the first few years. As we begin to mature, but before we develop our own sense of self, we
often find ourselves drawn too tightly to the people who have
wandered our way and stayed a while. That's a normal response.
But break away we must. We owe it to ourselves, to our loved
ones, even to the strangers among us. Each one of us must travel
our own unique, though complementary, path. Only in this way
can we add true benefit to the world around us. Only in this
way can we fulfill the will that is God's.

◆

Giving to those we walk among is why we are here. Making
sure we give what is ours to give and not trying to give that
which specifically belongs to others is crucial. Each one of us
is necessary to the completion of the journey.

THE FIRST TIME I HEARD PEOPLE TALKING ABOUT THE importance of having boundaries was in a Twelve Step meeting, and I was pretty confused. It was a term I was unfamiliar with, and even as I heard people share, I didn't understand their terminology or what they were distressed about. To me, a boundary meant something physical, like the hedges that separated the properties in many neighborhoods. But I knew this wasn't the meaning they were referring to.

After listening to members of the group talk for the whole hour, I was finally able to glimpse that my life was being sabotaged by the unclear boundaries between me and others. I realized that this was how I had always lived, in fact. I left the meeting not knowing if I would or should return.

I had never sought boundaries before this time. I had preferred enmeshment, actually. It meant you needed me, that I was the center of your life. Boundaries meant we were unnecessary to each other, and I was terrified of being unnecessary. That was how my life had felt for decades, and I had tried for years to deaden the pain of being invisible. My lack of success was what brought me into the very Twelve Step meeting where I heard about boundaries for the first time. The dilemma was unavoidable; I wanted to live without pain, but how?

I look back on this first meeting as God's answer to my search for freedom from the pain that had haunted me for years. We are always being led to the place where wisdom awaits us if we believe in the possibility that there is a solution that's perfect for us.

✦

I believe that respecting the boundaries between us is
what actually allows us to come together in ways that really
matter. We are students and teachers interchangeably, but
we must not blur the lines between us.

### Detachment is freedom from the desire to get someone back.

THERE ARE MANY REASONS WE MAY WANT TO VERBALLY attack someone. Perhaps we felt put down or embarrassed by something a co=worker said to us or about us when we were not present. Or a friend quite unexpectedly excluded us from an event she was planning that included all our mutual friends. Maybe we got wind of a rumor that was being spread about us, a vicious one in fact, and wholly untrue. In all these instances and many more, the urge to get back at the person who nailed us is powerful. Our ego is easily engaged by the ego attack of another. Accepting that this is a normal reaction is important. However, we don't want to stay in that frame of mind. This is even more important.

As children we are quick to fight back. Perhaps we are even encouraged to do so. Many parents push their children to be tough and to stand up to the classroom bully. It's not an easy les= son to learn that what we may have had to do in childhood to survive is not what we need to do as adults. Allowing others to have their say, regardless of what it is and knowing that it doesn't define us, is freedom at its finest. We don't get to that awareness immediately. It generally takes many experiences with multiple people to see that letting someone have their say, whatever it may be, is far more pleasant than doing battle with them. Letting others think whatever they want to think, or do whatever they want to do, are marvelous gifts to us. Being unburdened by the need to interact over every little experience that comes our way gives us so much extra time to simply enjoy being alive.

*

It's the little freedoms that count the most as we age, and this is one of them. Enjoy it to the fullest.

MANY WOULD ARGUE THAT WE CAN'T KEEP OUR FEELINGS separate from the actions of others or the circumstances that have befallen us. I am certainly not trying to convince you that this is an easy task, but it is doable. While I admit it has taken me hundreds of practice sessions, and the willingness, again and again, to look the other way, to turn a deaf ear, to let others have their own meltdowns and ego attacks without me getting ensnared, it is possible. And it feels so good when we succeed!

Accepting our powerlessness over the behavior of others isn't easy. We think, *If only I'd said it this way.* Or perhaps, *If only I had made that special dinner or brought flowers first.* We get fooled into thinking that if *we* do something differently, we might get the object of our attention to do something differently, too. Alas, that's never going to happen, unless by accident. People do what they do. Period. Our good fortune is to learn how empowered we feel when we let them!

Awaking each morning, being grateful to know that we can have the kind of day we want, is one of the gifts of embracing a spiritual program. Relieving ourselves of the burden of trying to make others conform to our wishes is a gift we can gladly unwrap a day at a time.

◆

Today promises to be a happy one, regardless of what
others are doing, if we are attending to our own business
and no one else's.

WE ARE SO PRACTICED AT TRYING TO CONTROL OTHERS.
We learn to be very subtle, certain that others can't detect our
efforts. But they can. I was a master at control, I thought. But all
I was really a master at was frustrating others and then myself too
with my lack of success. I was slow to learn that my attempts to
control were the result of my insecurities. I didn't want to admit
to being insecure; I thought it made me boring. How could I
be the one you wanted to be with if I was boring? I was a very
sick puppy until I finally found freedom from my obsession to
control those around me.

The freedom I finally found took years of diligence to realize.
That's the not-so-good news. It doesn't happen quickly, but it
will happen. Yet, vigilance will always be necessary. I have come
to believe that if I had mastered letting go of control in the first
attempt, I wouldn't have appreciated, nearly so much, the relief
I eventually enjoyed. But we get only a daily reprieve from the
obsession to control. The Serenity Prayer, with its suggestion to
accept those things we cannot change, is the moment's reminder
that sets our mind straight.

Whenever your focus is on what others are doing, pause. Take
a deep breath. Are you minding their business? Are you about
to say something that's better left unsaid? Is it time to back off
and refocus on the only business that matters, yours? Even the
thought that others should be doing something different is a
red flag. The time we have to do what needs to be done by us
will expand greatly when we allow others to live their own lives
while we attend to ours.

✦

We will be able to care so much more about the things that
really matter in our own lives when we let other people
attend to that which matters to them. Freeing our minds
offers so many unexpected gifts, the first of which is peace.

# pause *and* reflect

Backing away from an invitation to get involved in the affairs
of someone else is smart.

What someone else is doing or how they treat us has nothing
to do with who we are.

Witnessing for others may well be the kindest gift we can
offer. That act frees us from any form of interference.

Get over getting someone back! Now. We will never find
peace unless we do.

Our lives can be so much simpler than we make them.
After having read ninety essays, can you judge a change
in yourself? Can you see where some more willingness
might be necessary? Share your reflections with a friend.
Write about them and about where you'd like to take
your life next.

Learning, as I finally have, that what anyone does
doesn't define me has transformed my life. Are you feeling
a transformation in the making too? If so, please cherish
it enough to add some words about this in your journal.

# Detachment is not letting anyone else decide how you feel.

EVERYONE ELSE DECIDED HOW I FELT FOR MUCH OF THE first forty years of my life. It's embarrassing to admit this, and seeing it in print is even more discomfiting. But I can't escape who I was. Owning who we are, *or were,* throughout our lifetime is necessary if we want to embrace becoming someone who has another set of characteristics. Few of us will choose to stay as we were as youngsters for our entire lives; however, many of us will fear making changes of any consequence as adults. I definitely fell into this category.

I still remember so clearly trying to guess what was in someone else's mind so what was in mine could mirror it. This way I was certain to be in that person's favor. I had no idea who I was or who I wanted to be, other than a shadow of someone else. Was I always this way? I really don't know. I do have a glimmering of having dreams for myself as a young girl, dreams that didn't rely on others. I wrote short stories and plays in elementary school in which I solved mysteries and discovered clues no one else could find. I don't know where that girl went, but by junior high she was gone. From then on, I got quiet and tried to fit in. That's all. And I hoped others would not reject me. If the people around me didn't show warm approval, I was crushed. The pain of that period was daunting, but during that time I finally learned to turn to God, and that was the lesson I needed.

I look back over my life, as you do yours, no doubt, and wonder how I got from there to here. But I know, as do you, that where we are now is where our next lessons lie. We don't have to be afraid. Our lessons have waited for us, and we can handle whatever comes. We always did and we always will.

✦

No longer does anyone else have the power to control how I feel. The same is true for you. We get to decide that for ourselves. Isn't this a great and wonderful gift?

Detachment is freedom from saying,
"I told you so."

THE NEED TO BE RIGHT AND TO POINT THAT OUT IS EX-
tremely seductive. It's not that being right is inherently flawed.
But insisting that one is right emphatically implies that the other
person is wrong, and no one wants to be labeled in that way. It's
important to allow one another to save face in all interactions.

Any two people in any conversation will quite likely have
different perspectives on the topic being discussed, at times radi-
cally different. That makes for a very good conversation in most
instances. Being introduced to a new way of seeing a situation is
how we learn and grow. But if we are struggling to feel comfortable in our own skin, we may take exception to a viewpoint that
puts ours at risk. We may see the other viewpoint as diminishing
us and the other person as a bully of sorts. Fortunately, we can
learn how to take differing perspectives in stride. Even more
than that, we can see them as shortcuts to expanding our own
breadth of understanding about how life works.

None of us has every piece of this puzzle called life. But each
one of us is supplying different pieces in every conversation
we are having. That all the input in each conversation is what
expands the minds of every one of us is the greatest gift that
results from human interaction. Knowing that we need all the
input—all of it—will allow us to refrain from insisting that our
input is all that's valuable.

✦

Needing one another, wholly, is such a blessing. And
needing one another never means being more right in
any conversation. It means, "thank you for your thoughts."
Nothing more.

## 93   Detachment is being able to put yourself at the top of the list of "who needs care."

WANTING TO BE HELPFUL TO TRAVELERS SHARING OUR journey is not simply altruism. It's kind and appropriate. We are in each other's life quite intentionally, as has been said before. As the very wise people who speak for many spiritual philosophies would say, we must give away that which we also want to keep. But caring for others should not preclude making certain we have not forgotten ourselves. Self-care needs to be at the top of one's list, or we will fail to be present in crucial ways to all who seek our help and attention at any moment along the journey.

There are so many ways we need to care for ourselves. Getting enough rest is mandatory; exercise and healthy eating are necessary, too. Allowing for times alone with God or whomever we commune with as a spiritual practice ensures that we will have the focus and energy we need to do what really needs to be done. Having downtime to simply listen to the sounds around us and witness the colors in the landscape will offer us much quiet pleasure from which we can draw the energy needed to then witness the needs of those who walk with us, by intention.

Detaching from others and putting our needs first isn't selfish. It's being respectful of ourselves, which then allows us to respect others. We can't respect others without first meeting our own needs.

✦

Paying attention to our own needs is not selfish, but we may need to be reminded of that with some frequency. Wanting to be present to others is kind and extremely important. It's also a gift that honors the giver as well as the receiver.

I WONDER IF OTHER PEOPLE STRUGGLED AS MUCH AS I struggled for so many years to simply let others *be*. Why someone else's behavior or demeanor affected me so much continues to plague me when I'm in that space of self-doubt. Was this a lesson I specifically choose *before coming here?* Or did I simply misread the normal give-and-take that occurs between two people as evidence that I needed to do something different to make them and me all right and more comfortably in sync, fulfilling a sense of intimacy that I craved?

I don't really need to answer this question, I've decided, but I do need to apply, on a nearly constant basis, what I have come to cherish as the "need to know" rule. How others are behaving is entirely of their own choosing, and if they need input from me, they can ask for it. What they are doing does not reflect on me; it doesn't mean I am more or less worthy; it doesn't mean my input is necessary at all. There are two kinds of business, remember: my business and none of my business. There is never confusion about where one's attention should be. Never.

The "need to know" rule is the best of all shorthands to having a peaceful, free life. Others are on a journey, the intricacies of which we will never understand. And that is as it should be. Our own journey is enough for one mind to handle.

✦

Letting others *be* is such freedom once we get the full benefit of what it can feel like. It's not our natural inclination, initially, but it can become so with willingness.

Detachment means acknowledging and even celebrating another's unique journey.

WE AREN'T TRAVELING SIDE BY SIDE IN ORDER TO KEEP tabs on each other, although the impulse to do so may be great. Getting sucked into someone else's journey is powerful and can become a habitual, always unhealthy response. And it's never our purpose here to be in charge of someone else. Our own life slides quietly by when we are obsessing over how someone else is living theirs.

Time has been a good teacher for me, however. Time, coupled with the daily application of the principles I learned in Twelve Step rooms—principles that have changed every aspect of how I see my life and how I see the others in my life too—have offered me a freedom and a trust in God as the true orchestrator, not only for my life *but for your life too*.

Trust is the key word in allowing others to enjoy their own journeys. Believing, as I have come to believe, that no experience is accidental and no person has appeared without a prior invitation means I can trust that everyone else's journey is exactly as it has been ordered to be. And I am not the one who ordered it! My presence on the scene is to acknowledge it, that's all. This is a big relief, isn't it? We are where we are, doing what we are doing, appreciating one another as witnesses to the journey. What could be better than that? And what could be more important?

✦

Standing off to the side and appreciating the joy or being present for the sorrow of another person's life is the most important gift we can ever offer someone. Trusting that wherever we are is the place where we can do this best simplifies our life.

Detachment is no longer "dancing"
around someone else's life.

WANTING TO BE CENTRAL TO SOMEONE ELSE'S LIFE OR
wanting someone else to be the exclusive core of your life are
common traits of the classic codependent. It's an extremely
restrictive way to live, one that doesn't allow for the kind of
spontaneity that is necessary if we are to attentively greet the
lessons for which we have been waiting and prepared. Dancing
around others means we are paying attention primarily to their
lives, not to our own. We are living in *their* present moment,
not our own.

Most of us do this at some point, maybe even for an extended
period of time. But the sooner we see the downside of living
another's person's present moment and start living our own, the
sooner we will discover the real peace and joy we have come
here to experience.

We can appreciate the lives that others are experiencing; indeed, that's honoring them in an important way, and we can
even be dance partners in our shared moments. We simply can't
lay aside our own present moments and the lessons contained
within them, and expect to live to our fullest potential, an expectation that is ingrained in us and, if ignored, will cause us
*dis*-ease.

It's not easy to detach, to live only our own life and yet remain a part of the community around us. But we can learn how
to respect, appreciate, and honor one another without being
subsumed by the dance another person must do. When we discover how easy it is to live *alongside* our loved ones, we will grow
in our appreciation of their moments right along with our own.

✦

Loving the moment we are living right now is the kindest
way to spend our life. It will teach us everything we need to
know and will give us every opportunity we need to dance
the dance that is ours and only ours.

## Detachment is no longer needing to assuage anyone else's anger.

BECAUSE I GREW UP IN A HOUSEHOLD WHERE ANGER WAS a dominant theme, I learned to slip away, emotionally and physically, so that I didn't become the brunt of it. I also became very practiced at trying to relieve the aftereffects. Although I did come to understand the physic impetus for the anger, my education didn't come soon enough. Thus, for far too many years I *practiced anger* myself. We do learn how to be by what we see.

It became second nature to me to either be angry or to try to alleviate someone else's anger. Either way, the underlying fear I had about living, day to day, was overwhelming. The fireball of anxiety I experienced from childhood until my forties prompted many reactions from me in all my primary relationships, and few of those reactions were pretty. My relationships were fraught with struggle because of my attempts to fix situations, to change a person, or to plead for forgiveness and acceptance. My fear of rejection was all-consuming at times, so I used all these responses interchangeably. As I recount these things from my past, I stand amazed that who I was has become who I now am. That's the very good news for all of us: we all are works in progress.

Being able to let others have their feelings, regardless of what those feelings are, is perhaps the greatest gift we can offer ourselves on a daily basis. While it's true that some feelings expressed by others are easier to walk away from than anger, all feelings can be equally accepted if we remember what our real job is: detachment.

◆

Not needing to try to change anyone else allows us far more time to work on the details of our own lives. And that's quite enough for any one person.

NONE OF US IS BEYOND BEING INFLUENCED BY THE PRES-
ence of others: their traits, their opinions, their speech patterns,
even their mannerisms. And there is nothing wrong with adopting some of the characteristics of others as our own. It has been
said that imitation is the highest form of flattery. But letting the
behavior of others determine our own behavior in every respect
means we are hollow shells, simply waiting for the presence of
others to determine who we will be in the next moment.

It's not always easy to figure out who we want to be, particularly if we grew up in a family that didn't encourage self-
exploration or self-expression. But it's never too late to imagine
a new kind of life for ourselves, a new kind of commitment for
the future we'd like to experience. What will unfold, eventually,
is what we expect. Our minds are powerful. We can change how
we see our lives as well as how we live them by a simple change
of attitude, here and now.

How exciting to realize that no one is holding us back any
more but ourselves. If we want to make waves, we can. If we
want to depart from who we have been, even for decades, we
can. If we want to create an entirely new persona, we have the
right to do that too. Our dreams are the only materials we need
to fashion a new beginning.

✦

Having a dream for where to go next is the first major step
to getting there. It's never too late to learn to dream. Never.

## 99    Detachment is accepting what we cannot change and changing only what we can.

THIS PRINCIPLE HAS A FAMILIAR RING TO IT, DOESN'T IT? It sounds a bit like the Serenity Prayer. Knowing the difference between what we can change and what's not our business to try to change makes the difference between having a peaceful moment or a frustrating one. The pull to try to change others can be excruciatingly strong, particularly if we have convinced ourselves that we did it successfully in the past. But we did no such thing. Others might have changed, and they might have done exactly as we'd hoped, but it wasn't because of us. People change only because they see a benefit in it.

Having assumed success in the past is an unfortunate assumption because it seduces us into continuing our efforts to control the behaviors of others in the present. Everyone becomes frustrated when this is the approach we take in our relationships. Control never bares fruit for long, and it will always cause conflict and pain.

Coming to appreciate the freedom we get when we detach, when we give up the attempt to change others, is not immediate perhaps, but the more we practice looking the other way when others are present, the greater will be our own peace of mind. It comes incrementally. And every peaceful moment will serve as the carrot to lead us to make this choice again and again. Everyone wants to know peace. We can be peacemakers by backing off when our own business isn't central to the activity before us.

◆

Detachment is the solution to most of our relationship problems. Actually, I am inclined to say all of them, but absolutes can be hard to fathom. Just trust that letting go is the way to go.

MANY OF US WERE RAISED IN HOMES REPLETE WITH ANGST
and strife, where it was difficult to discern the line between *their*
words and actions and *our* worthiness. In many instances, there
was no line. We were scapegoats for all the problems that sur-
faced in the family. That characterization may have followed you
into relationship after relationship. That's not unusual. But it's
not how you have to perceive yourself for the rest of your life.
Having chosen this book to read suggests that if this has been
your life story up to now, you are committed to changing it,
from this day forward. Hallelujah!

The behavior we experience or observe up close or even
from afar need not reflect on us. That's not an easy idea to inter-
nalize, perhaps. I, for one, lived many decades of my life letting
others' behavior dictate who I was and how I should feel. My
self-esteem was deplorable. Did others expect me to absorb their
outbursts? I don't think so, but my family of origin had passed
on to me that which they had learned from their parents. That's
how the torch gets passed. Another person's behavior defined
them. Period. Taking what they do as an assessment of who we
are is missing the entire point of why we are sharing the journey.

We share the journey to learn from one another—to live in
concert but not in the shadow of one another. To join our minds
in the moment for the sheer joy of connection. That is the main
reason to be grateful, in fact. We are here as way-showers and
companions. Let's stick with that and nothing more.

✦

> Others do what they do because of who they are and the
> journey they are on. It's our opportunity to observe from
> afar or up close, knowing that we can share a moment
> and then move on to the next moment and the gift it is
> waiting to offer.

# pause *and* reflect

> Caring first for ourselves, rather than others, is not
> being selfish.
> Giving up control over someone else takes more than just
> wishing it. Much more.
> Everyone's journey is unique to them. When we interfere, we
> delay their process.
> Letting someone else be angry is a sign of growth
> and freedom.

Our interactions with others are specific to the needs
we have. They are the lessons we have requested at some
earlier time and place. Is there a lesson that you recently
had which still troubles you? Have you gone to God for
clarification? Seek the silence for your answers.

How many times of late have you allowed those around
you to express whatever feeling was in their minds? Every
time we let others be themselves, we get the fruits of freedom ourselves. And God appreciates our noninvolvement.

These are areas that deserve some reflection. Take some
time away and write about these ideas. Tomorrow, read
what you wrote today.

BEING AT THE MERCY OF THE MANY INDIVIDUALS WHO will cross our path on any single day is simply exhausting. Some people will be kind; with them our interactions will be pleasant. Others will be dismissive. Many will choose not to hear us, regardless of what we are saying, and we will feel judged. A few will be genuinely grateful that we are sharing their journeys, and their response to us will make us feel appreciated and energized.

Because of these varied responses, however, we must not get caught in the web of letting how anyone receives us determine how we feel or how we might determine our next move. Waiting for anyone to treat us well is like waiting for the sun to come out on a cloudy day. We can't control the behavior of others. We can decide our own best response to every situation, though, and that means we are free from the effects of life's uncertainties.

Choosing our own reactions, our own thoughts in every encounter, will empower us to meet any circumstance that comes our way—circumstances that some spiritual teachers would say we have invited for the lessons they offer. Getting a taste of empowerment is all it takes for most of us to refrain from allowing the behavior of others to define us. I never thought I could master this tool, but I have. So can you!

◆

There is not a direct correlation between what someone else does and what you and I choose to do. Let's choose wisely and live more peacefully.

WHAT DOES IT MEAN TO LET THINGS REST? I DIDN'T GRASP this principle very quickly. I figured that if I presented my point of view, my judgment about anything, in a little different way, I'd be able to convince you that your way of thinking or seeing was faulty, or at the least, not as good as mine. I was often relentless. But no matter how persistent I was, I was not able to make others change. My family continued to favor their own opinions, my husband continued to drink, and my friends simply stayed away.

I'd like to say that now, after years of practicing a new way of living, I always let things rest after a first or second attempt to change someone's opinion, but that would be dishonest. Sometimes I still persist; occasionally I am still relentless. But I have made progress. That's all any of us can be certain of when we make the effort to change a behavior. Progress is actually the beginning of anyone's story of success. I am creating mine. With effort we can all do it.

✦

Letting things rest, surrendering to the Power guiding every one of us, offers such wonderfully relaxing, peaceful moments. Experiencing the joy of this even once a day is sure to convince us that making a practice of it will embolden us, day in and day out, to repeat it again and again.

Detachment is being able to move
our minds away from the unhealthy
places they want to go.

IT'S A THRILLING REALIZATION TO KNOW THAT WE ARE IN
control of our minds. For some, this comes as a surprise. Minds
just seem to contain information willy-nilly. I, for one, was quite
convinced for many years that others had the power to create,
maintain, or change the thoughts in my mind. I willingly gave
to others power over my mind on a regular basis. If someone
looked at me disapprovingly, or didn't notice me at all, which
was more often the case, I was shattered and my self-assessment
was rewritten.

The healthiest place for one's mind to be is on the power and
presence of God as we understand Him or Her. Keeping our
mind there means we will know the next right thing to say, the
next right thing to do, the next right and healthy thing to think.
But it's natural to wonder why our minds even want to dwell
in unhealthy places. I think the answer is that the ego is most
comfortable there and it has a stranglehold on many of us. The
ego's power to divert us from our true path is only as great as
our attention to that voice that hollers angry, negative directives.

There are two voices in our minds: a quiet, loving voice and
a loud, generally spiteful voice. The latter will always direct us
to the unhealthy places, but we can learn to detach from that
voice and to relish the quiet one instead. Prayer will always lead
us back to where we want to be.

+

Prayer is the answer in all stressful situations. We might not
get an answer right away, but we will get quiet relief from a
mind that is careening out of control. Praise be to God, as is
so often said.

Detachment is being able to stop
our minds in midthought when the
thoughts are not beneficial.

NOT BEING AT THE MERCY OF OUR THOUGHTS IS AKIN
to not being at the mercy of the reactions we get from others
regarding our thoughts. Our thoughts are what we have cre=
ated them to be, and it's foolish to ever say, "I can't help it, that's
just how I am," in regard to any thought or situation that has
ensnared us. Indeed, we have willingly adopted every thought
we harbor.

We are always very much in control of what we say, think,
and do. This idea has been expressed time and again in this book,
but it bears repeating because we are so quick to give in to the
idea that we can't take charge of who we are becoming. Every
thought we entertain is, in fact, molding us into the people we
are. We are works in progress, some say, and that's good: it means
we don't have to be perfect. Simply deciding to monitor our
thoughts, to change their focus, and to quash any one of them
that doesn't add to the peace and joy of the world around us
is an excellent contribution we might consider making on a
daily basis.

There is great joy in the practice of stopping a negative
thought midsentence and refocusing it. Not being in its clutches
gives us hope for any number of changes we might want to make
in our lives. This is a simple place to begin; our mind is con=
stantly thinking, after all. And we can be constantly refocusing.

◆

We might all agree that we harbor many not-so-beneficial
thoughts. That's the bad news, perhaps. But the story
doesn't end there, and that's the good news. We can change
our negative thoughts, one and all. Today is a great day to
begin the practice.

Detachment is no longer living in the
tumultuous spaces of other peoples' minds.

105

ONE OF THE FIRST THINGS HANDED TO ME BY MY SPONSOR
when I got sober was the AA acceptance pamphlet. She told
me, "Read it and believe every word; it will change your life." I
did read it, over and over; I even tucked it under my pillow. But
I still had trouble staying out of the minds of others. And I was
extremely good at letting those same others live, rent free, in my
mind. Discerning who I was and who others were had always
been blurred for me. I so wanted to belong that allowing myself
to live in the midst of others' minds and vice versa seemed better than not knowing where I lived at all. Fortunately, those days
are long gone now.

But when someone is vulnerable due to illness, lack of rest, an
unhealthy diet, an emotional upset of some kind, or even a mild
affront by a friend or partner, it's easy to fall back and repeat our
earlier responses to unfriendly situations confronting us. Climb-
ing back into someone else's mind isn't that difficult, unfortunately. Staying there for as long as we did before is unlikely,
however. That's the payoff from incorporating new information
and practicing a new set of behaviors.

To the uninitiated, accepting others as they are with no hope
of changing them may seem like a joyless way to live. But, on
the contrary, it's the only way to actually experience lasting joy.

◆

> I will let others be and enjoy them for who they are. My
> lesson is to let go. Every day, anew, this is the lesson:
> to let go.

Detachment doesn't mean separation
from our loved ones. It means
acceptance of who and what they are.

I used to think that detachment meant I had to
separate myself completely from the person who was getting too
much of my attention. I didn't seem able to let someone be in
my life without them taking over my life. Therefore, my only al-
ternative was to deny or ignore their presence altogether, which
meant I wasn't able to claim the lessons I had been destined to
receive from that person, lessons we had agreed on a long time
ago, according to Caroline Myss.

Our loved ones cry out to be accepted by us, and we resist
when we can't make them conform to our wishes. When we
refuse to accept people as they are, we are creating a separation
that breeds ill will along with illness. The desire, in fact the need,
to join with others lies deep within us, but we can deny that call.
And when we do, we fail ourselves, one another, and the entire
human community.

We so easily misconstrue the meaning of detachment. It's
not about denying the presence or the importance of anyone.
It's not about moving on without our loved ones. It's not about
judgment. Detachment is about taking care of ourselves and letting others do the same. Freedom for all is detachment in action.

◆

Detachment doesn't preclude joining with our loved ones.
But distinct separation will result in our relationships being
harmed. The better choice between the two is clearly
discernible.

MANY OF US GO THROUGH LIFE CONNECTED AT THE HIP, so to speak, with someone we consider special and "ours." If we aren't "attached" to someone, we feel unworthy. Our journey is about coming to understand that attaching ourselves to God is what promises us the worthiness and security we seek, and this realization will change every experience, every day.

God's grace, which is our gift, is what allows us to know and appreciate detachment. His grace moves us from where we are at any moment to a very soft and secure place. God's presence is certain. The presence of others can be fleeting.

Needing others on our journey does *not* mean that we are lesser beings and have no life of our own. Indeed, having a rich and full life of our own is the very gift we bring to those special relationships that attract our attention.

For decades I have pondered why so many feel that without a life partner they are nothing. The answer may vary for different people, but I think at one time in my life it was because I felt invisible, even among friends, and I wanted one person, at the very least, to make me feel important. So when that person showed up, I clung. My attachment suffocated him and the relationship. I was a very slow learner; I suffocated many before I learned the value of detachment. Now I treasure being able to let God give me all the comfort and security I need.

✦

Detachment is a gift that benefits everyone. Not being the constant focus of someone else is freeing. Not making someone else our "assignment" lets us live the life we are here to live.

# 108 Detachment never means being rude or dismissive.

FOR SOME, THE IDEA OF DETACHMENT MAY BE ELUSIVE. It's a word that's more common in some circles than others. When I first heard the term, I assumed that shunning others was a reasonable way to express detachment. I had no idea that it was actually an act of love. I thought criticism might fit with the idea of detachment, but seeing detachment as allowing a person to be who they needed to be, without interference, without being judged or put down or ignored, were all very new ideas for me to incorporate.

But I am incorporating them, and my life is being transformed. What a pleasure to make the decision to refrain from criticizing others for who they are. I can't say I succeed 100 percent of the time. But I am adding many moments of peace to the world I inhabit by the many times I choose to think a thought that pleases God, rather than one I might have chosen to think before being introduced to the principle of detachment. Initially, letting others be, without comment from me, is truly an act of will, but in time it becomes an act of choice. The benefits are immeasurable.

◆

Giving up being rude simplifies our lives. Letting God direct our thoughts simplifies them even more. It is God's hope that we let others be. That's detachment.

Detachment is a growth opportunity that
we can claim every day of our lives.

109

THE CELEBRATION OF DETACHMENT IS NOT WHAT I SOUGHT when first introduced to the concept. I didn't want to be *detached*, I wanted to be *attached*. To me, that meant I was "chosen," and there was really nothing more important to me at the time. Celebrating my life as a woman with specific gifts and goals didn't seem inclusive enough. I wanted others to be with me, living my life every step of the way for validation. Not until my forties did I see the value of living in concert, in sync, but not enmeshed with that special other person.

What I see now is that we can walk among others and have our own life intact. We can allow others to do and be whomever their Spirit is calling them to be. We can witness them but not expect them to turn their life and will over to us. This means we will be able to see all the other invitations that might be swimming our way. When we are too involved in the life of someone else, perhaps demanding that they be a constant part of our life, we will never experience the individual growth we deserve.

Being detached doesn't mean not caring. It doesn't mean feeling no connection to someone else. It is not a way to distance ourselves from others. It is an expression of honest love—for both of us in the relationship. This is such good news when we finally are able to hear it and absorb it. Witnessing is the gift; detachment is the tool.

◆

Are you ready to grow today in whatever way is calling you? Unless you are living a life free from the obsession with others, you will miss one opportunity after another, and most will never come again.

## Detachment is not to be confused with disloyalty.

TRUSTING IN THE PROCESS OF LETTING OTHERS HAVE THE growth they are here to experience is freedom for all concerned. Unfortunately, I have many memories of wanting to hold someone back from an experience they were ready for. My lack of trust in their process occurred because I didn't trust that my Higher Power was part of my process. I planned my life around them and if they were moving on, or if I was, what would happen to us?

Fortunately, I have finally claimed detachment as one of my most treasured assets. I am not always good at it; I do still want to control far too often. But I had to learn that detachment didn't mean turning my back on someone before I could learn to feel good about adding it to my repertoire of characteristics. It has freed me and my loved ones in ways that neither I nor they could have imagined.

I sometimes wonder how my earlier relationships might have fared had I known then what I love knowing and living now. But I do also believe that we are always where we need to be, learning the lessons we are ready for. In earlier relationships I simply wasn't ready for the information I now cherish. There is no need for remorse. We were only ready for what we were ready for.

✦

Deciding to trust that everyone has their own Higher Power frees us to listen to ours. We can't know what's right for someone else. And letting them find their own way, without our input, is not being disloyal; on the contrary, it's being respectful.

# pause and reflect

What a relief it is to let things be as they are.
Our minds only go where we give them permission to go.
Accepting others as they are feels like a holiday.
The practice of detaching does not mean being rude.
We can still be loyal to our friends and loved ones and detach
   from them.

It's not easy to fully grasp the concept of detachment. But by considering what attachment to others feels like, you can get a glimmering. Rest awhile in this awareness.

What do you most want to change about your relationships with others? Does the practice of detachment call to you in any way? Are your relationships clean and healthy now? If not, look at what you might change. Perhaps detaching from a loved one's journey will ultimately bring you closer. Think about this for a spell and then write about the thoughts that come to you.

Detachment from the problems of
others is God's will. They and God will
solve what needs to be solved.

REMEMBERING THAT EVERYONE HAS HIS OR HER OWN
Higher Power relieves us of so much stress. Taking on someone else's problems, even when they touch us in some way,
is not necessary. That's what God is for. God is waiting to be
called on. Our Higher Power is always just a prayer, an idea, or
a question away.

Why is this so hard to remember? Even after we glimpse the
power of this truth, we have to be willing to pray, asking God
for the help we need that has already been promised to us. God
knows our needs. But it's helpful for us to think them or voice
them so that we know them too. That way we can recognize
when the help has arrived.

The same is true for our companions. Their problems are for
God to solve. We are not participants in their solutions. We can
listen, we can share what has worked for us, we can pray with
them. But we are not here to convey God's will.

Watching others discover the power inherent in prayer lets
us witness the power inherent in our detachment from them as
they seek their own solutions. All of us are emboldened by the
success that any one of us has with both prayer and detachment.
Prayer and detachment complement each other.

◆

When we need guidance, we seek God's will. When we need
comfort, we seek God's presence. When we seem called to
solve a problem for someone else, we let them go to God. In
that way, all will be served.

HOW DOES STAYING UNINVOLVED WITH THE SITUATIONS
in others' lives seem loving? I spent years assuming the opposite
was true. I was very clever at wiggling my way into one life or
another. Not being involved with the problems of the many
people on my path felt unsympathetic and selfish. It also felt
lonely. Perhaps my loneliness was what truly initiated my clinging to others.

Being told that detaching from the lives of others, their problems, and their cries for help is the best, most loving response
we can make seems farfetched, doesn't it? It took the wisdom of
many voices to convince me that this was my best response to
the people and situations I so frequently found myself in.

I do think we find ourselves in circumstances where we can
best learn what's needed for the next leg of our journey. I can't
be more grateful than I am for having learned the joy that accompanies the act of detachment. To be honest, at one time
I didn't think detaching from the lives or problems of others
was ever going to be worth my effort. How wrong I was. It
has taught me love—how to express it, how to receive it, how
to savor it.

◆

Love comes in many forms. One of the most helpful forms
for all the companions we will know today or any day
is detachment. It's what gives us the most freedom and
ultimately the most wisdom too. God lives in the tiny spaces
of our letting go.

WE ALL HAVE DREAMS. SOME OF US HAVE BIGGER DREAMS than others. My husband's was to build an experimental aircraft, which he is currently doing. I have one friend whose dream is to run a marathon, and she is training for her first one at age sixty-one. My aunt's dream was to live until she was one hundred. She made it, just shy by two months, but she told us all she was one hundred anyway. In her mind, she had made it. And my mother's dream was to learn to drive; at age fifty-two she took lessons, secretly, and surprised all of us.

My dream is to continue writing until the day I die. I am reminded of Frida Kahlo and how she painted lying down when she was in too much pain to stand or sit. It was her dream to simply keep painting.

The dream that any one of us has can best come to fruition if we have clear boundaries between what is ours to do and what belongs to others. When the boundaries are clear, we are empowered to follow our passions. We simply can't follow our bliss if we are tied to the dreams or problems of others. Therefore, detachment is a necessary tool and one that we must practice repeatedly if we really want to fulfill our own dreams.

Remember, when someone else is following his or her own bliss, it does not mean we don't matter to them. It's really a gift for any of us to follow our own bliss. Likewise, others are still important to us when we are following our dream. But our minds can't be two places at once.

◆

Dreams are meant to be fulfilled. That's why they have visited us. The only thing standing in our way is our over-involvement in the lives of others. Detach and watch the dream unfold.

To blame others for what is not going right in our life is such a temptation. I blamed others for years. I saw it practiced in my home and with friends. It simply became habitual, thoughtlessly habitual, and it's a very difficult habit to break. What has successfully worked for me, much of the time, is the decision to remain quiet, to detach from the person or the situation that is getting under my skin. I didn't believe this choice was a viable one for many years. It did take focused effort and many hours of practice—many *years* of practice. But I have made progress.

Choosing to forego blame actually feels very good. Taking responsibility for what we have done and letting others off the hook when they aren't ready to do the same is really very freeing. Having made a practice of letting others do and be whatever appeals to them is a gift to ourselves and to them, a gift that simply changes every aspect of our journey.

We are here to watch and learn. We are here to bless and witness. We are here to offer guidance when sought. We are here to share our experience, strength, and hope. Our purpose is never to blame. Everyone is stuck in an old perspective, a place where growth can't happen, if we are caught in the web of blaming.

◆

We can break free from blaming any time we want. The door to a new way of seeing and behaving is always open.

THIS MAY SEEM LIKE AN UNUSUAL WAY TO DESCRIBE DE-
tachment, but when I practice detachment, it feels as though I
am letting my shoulders relax and simply breathing deeply after
trying to hold on to the unmanageable. Hanging on to others,
in any fashion, will never be successful. We can't hold back their
minds, their actions, their opinions. Letting go of every aspect of
whom someone else chooses to be is not easy, but it's so rewarding, once we get accustomed to it.

It makes our own lives so much simpler when we let those
who walk among us do whatever they want to do. Now, of
course, when our offspring are young, we can't let them be un-
supervised. But it's folly to think that we will be able to control
their every move. Their own free will will surface quite regularly,
just as ours continues to do. But our acknowledging that it's
okay for them and all others to listen to guiding voices different from our own results in many opportunities for gratitude.
Being grateful for even the tiny experiences that we have with
letting others be, letting others do that which they feel called to
do, even if it proves to be wrong in the long run, is the breath
of fresh air we deserve.

There are many gifts that come with detachment. Relaxation
is one of them. Freedom from stress is another. A quiet mind
is perhaps the best of all. Gratitude becomes all-encompassing
when we really let others live their own lives. I am so glad I
made a commitment to this practice.

✦

The commitment to detach from the lives of others begins
with a decision. It's a decision we can make moment by
moment. Yet it is life changing.

Prayer is an effective way to help us
detach from the behavior of others.

116

WE CAN ONLY HOLD ON TO ONE THOUGHT AT A TIME.
Making the one thought we are dwelling on a prayer in a time
of turmoil means we can't be thinking that someone ought to
be doing something they aren't currently doing. This is a great
shorthand way of changing who we are and how every moment
feels. This is not to imply that we need to be in silent repose
all day. But rather, when we begin to harbor thoughts about
anyone else, thoughts that aren't loving, gentle, and accepting,
it's time to ask God for another thought. Prayer can be quick
and simple. We can do it with our eyes open as well as closed.

Knowing that detachment happens most effectively when we
are in partnership with God gives me great relief. There are simply too many things that are hard to handle all alone. And what
I've learned from my many years on this spiritual path is that
none of them will be very effectively translated into a peaceful
life if I ignore the help from God, as I understand Him or Her,
that's available just as soon as I seek it.

It's important to acknowledge the many others who are traveling with me, too. They are not accidental travelers accom-
panying me on this path. It's by design; it's all by design. And
that's the best news of all. It makes detachment even easier, don't
you agree?

◆

Prayer is the solution. Detachment is the tool. Peace of mind
is the gift.

CHOOSING A RIGHT ACTION IS ALWAYS PREFERABLE TO falling into an automatic reaction. But the latter is the more common response for many of us. For years, I constantly re-acted to what people were doing or saying. I reacted to their opinions and tried to make mine similar where possible or to convince them to change theirs. I made many important deci-sions about very personal details of my life in reaction to the decisions others were making. I didn't take stock of me and what I wanted. Frankly, I wasn't sure how one did that. I tried to be what someone else thought I should be. It got me drunk. It got me divorced! It got me depressed, lonely, and confused.

Not everyone has had results like mine, perhaps, but no one has a fully productive or peaceful life if they are simply trying to fit in in order to be accepted. Perhaps growing up in a fam-ily that didn't value independence contributed to my codepen-dency regarding the opinions and actions of others. But there is no blame to be laid. I did what I did. And I'd say the end result has been very good.

It's interesting how we end up where we actually need to be. Writing this book and the many that preceded it are the results of the many struggles I had. Today I can truly say that I am grateful. I am also truly grateful to have learned the true nature and value of detachment. I know, without contradiction, that practicing detachment is the only way I can fully live the life I am here to live.

✦

Reacting to others is exhausting, in the final analysis. And it's habitual. But so is the practice of detachment, and it's guaranteed to make us feel peaceful.

When we practice detachment, we serve as great teachers to others.

118

WE ARE REMINDED IN THE WORDS OF MANY SPIRITUAL guides that we are in the role of either teacher or student in every moment of time. And we switch, rather quietly, between one and the other. It's probable that we aren't even certain which role we are in at a particular time; the difference between the two is subtle. But also, we don't necessarily know what our companion has been sent to learn.

Modeling detachment, however, is one of the most important tools we can pass on to others, regardless of who our companions are. It's not that we should be unaffected or uninfluenced by those around us, particularly when acts of love and gratitude are being expressed. But allowing behavior of any kind to determine how we feel makes us constantly dependent on others. As I've already said, we do share a path with people we need to learn from, but the path we share is a two-way street. We are both giving and receiving from one another. Constantly.

The idea of practicing detachment is such a gentle one, isn't it? It allows us to be imperfect. Because we don't detach perfectly, even for a few hours at a time, we can begin again the next day. No harm has been done, really. We can forgive ourselves for going where we didn't need to go, and then take each new experience as it presents itself and practice detachment again, one experience and one person at a time.

◆

The freedom we are promised when we practice detachment is unfathomable to most. We must experience it in order to believe it. Perhaps today is a good day to begin making the changes that will really matter in our lives tomorrow.

### If we become too detached, will others leave us behind?

CLINGING IN ORDER TO KEEP A PARTNER FROM STRAYING is common to many. But since fear drives this kind of behavior, it really doesn't prevent the very thing we are afraid of; in fact, it might even trigger it. Not only have I had personal experience with this, but I have known dozens of others who have been certain that the right word, the right action or reaction, or the right gift would make another feel indebted for life. But to no avail. In other words, attachment does not prevent a person from leaving. This brings us to detachment.

Will the expression of detachment, boldly stated by one's actions, lead to being left behind? I certainly can't answer this with absolute assurance, but my experience, my interactions with others on many levels, my path of spiritual enlightenment, have led me to believe that people leave because they must. It's not what we do or say that drives a person away. What one has needed to learn has been learned, and the time is right to move on.

This might seem to be a cold assessment, but I think that looking at this principle objectively allows us to see that there is usually no harm intended, not really, when one moves on. Our commitment to detachment allows us to let others go without our feeling so personally rejected. Our teachers are everywhere. Learning to say good-bye, without rancor, is growth.

◆

Detachment doesn't push people away. It frees all of us. Let's not forget that.

The most loving thing we can do is let
another person be free; that's detachment.

120

BUYING FLOWERS FOR A FRIEND IS CERTAINLY LOVING. SO is buying lunch for a special occasion. Making a phone call or sending an email just to say hello is a sign of caring too. There are multiple ways of expressing love, many of which we utilize regularly. But letting someone go, to be free to do whatever they want to do, which may be the hardest of all our expressions, is the clearest sign of love we can offer. It says, "I trust you to do what you need to do."

It's not easy to detach from the movements of others. Far too often we rely on their presence to complete us. But holding someone back from the experiences they be ready for puts us in charge of another's growth. It's a behavior that will also come back to bite us if the person misses an opportunity that they have longed for. We simply must let people evolve as they desire. That doesn't mean they might not get burned, but at least we are not holding the flame.

Detaching from the changes others may need to make may never be easy, at least not initially. But it does get easier. And it does feel better than clinging to the object of our affection. We can't have the life we need if we are too wrapped up in the life someone else needs. Letting them go accomplishes two things: it allows us and the other person to soar.

✦

We may not realize that we also need to be free, but when we begin to experience it on a more regular basis we will realize what we had been missing. And we will not want to go back to the way things were before.

# pause *and* reflect

Let go of the opinions of others.
Let go of the effect of your behavior on others.
Let go of the outcome of your actions and the many
situations concerning you and your loved ones.

Do you currently practice any trait that empowers you? If you do, recount in your journal how that came about. If you don't, consider the benefits of detachment. You will feel like a new, quite powerful person, one who has taken charge of herself.

Take a moment every morning to envision yourself as a self-directed person. Being self-directed does not mean being selfish, nor does it mean ignoring others. Write in your journal what it does mean to you.

How does letting go feel to you? Share in your journal or with a friend. Is it a trait you cherish?

IT HAS NOT BEEN MY EXPERIENCE TO PERFECT DETACH-
ment after only one try. For me, detachment has been similar to
seeking God's will: I have needed to do it every day, many times
a day. It's akin to practicing any new exercise. It's not mysterious,
really; it just feels unnatural at first. We are inclined to interfere
in the business of others, but detachment closes that door. It
follows on the heels of a decision, and one that empowers us
a tiny bit more every time we make it. We must be willing to
make it, however.

If we want to change how life feels, we have to be willing
to change an aspect of our behavior because if we continue to
do what we have always done, we will most likely continue to
experience what we have always experienced. Detaching from
those people who get under our skin, or from those situations
we feel compelled to try to control, is committing to a specific
change in behavior. But how do we do it? That's the niggling
question for most of us. But I have some reasonable suggestions.

We detach in steps. The first step is to observe but say nothing. The second step is to say a quiet prayer and then avert our
eyes, placing our mind with God and some details of our own
life. The third step is to get busy, to move on, and to thank God
for giving us the willingness to let others do what they need
to do. All these steps will need repeated practice; at least I have
found that to be the case. But each time I have walked myself
through them, I have felt empowered and hopeful, and that has
made me willing to take the walk the next time too.

◆

One moment at a time is how we live. So it makes sense
that we can only detach one moment at a time too. What's
stopping you from trying?

LETTING OTHERS BE ACCOUNTABLE FOR THEMSELVES MEANS
we are relinquishing our need to assume responsibility for those
actions and situations that clearly are not ours to manage. The
attraction to be overly responsible is so great, however, and what
makes it even greater is our lack of trust in any outcome we
aren't part of.

Our fear about our future seduces us into thinking that if
we could only ensnare our partners in our own very special
web, taking responsibility for their lives along with our own,
we'd be secure. But, as I've said, we cannot be even moderately
responsible and attentive to our own very specific work if we
are focusing on the work someone else is here to do. We can
work in tandem with others, and in many instances should, but
crossing the boundary between us that needs to be honored will
eventually imprison us.

Learning how to be accountable is like learning any trait.
Most of us aren't born with a natural inclination for it, but modeling the behavior of those people among us who seem to be
peaceful might be one way to learn it. What we will see, with
careful observation, is that letting others be wholly responsible
and accountable for themselves appears to make folks feel good.
Deciding we want to feel good is one of the most sensible reasons for adopting this practice.

◆

Being accountable builds self-worth. It helps others to
be able to trust us. Letting the people around us become
accountable is one of the best gifts we can give them. Our
doing for others what needs to be done by them will stunt
their growth. Let's not be guilty of that.

Detachment is the way to cultivate
peace, one moment at a time.

123

I CLAIM I WANT TO BE PEACEFUL ALL THE TIME, YET I generally spend some hours every day in a space that's not particularly peaceful. And it's always for the same reason: I have placed my attention where it doesn't belong, on situations that don't really concern me. I am drawn like a moth to a flame when my loved ones (sometimes even strangers) are fussing over matters that trouble them. I read the signs and assume I am needed to resolve their problem. Sound familiar?

Turning away seems impossible if the person being affected is someone truly significant to me. But that's the very time I most need to do so. My primary role in anyone's life is to witness what their experience is, to offer suggestions only when they are sought, and to pray that all will be well and that the lesson they need is forthcoming. Each time I can practice any one of these responses, I will discover peace. And as the waves of peace wash over me, I will know, for certain, that I am fulfilling God's will in that moment.

Peace, however it visits us, feels so good. Wanting to capture it for longer spells is natural, and knowing that we can do so, by making the decision to observe and then turn away from situations that are not ours to resolve, makes the peaceful wave more than a wish. It can become our reality.

◆

To cultivate peace requires us to make some decisions.
We need to give up our need to manage anyone else's life.
We decide, instead, to address only those situations that
are obviously ours, and then we pray for the willingness
to do both.

Those who are hardest to detach
from are our best teachers.

I DON'T NEED TO REMIND YOU THAT WE ARE SERVING AS teachers and students, interchangeably, all the time. But when we are in the midst of a conflict with someone over how a situation should be managed, we so easily forget those things that have given us strength and peace in the past. A conflict always means that a teaching and learning opportunity is presenting itself. In most cases, both sides need to detach; both sides can learn as well as teach. And if detachment is explored by one side or the other, both people will gain some moments of peace. It takes at least two to have a conflict, remember.

It's been my experience that the people I care most about are hardest to detach from. Perhaps I am too invested emotionally to walk away when I should. But I have learned, with practice, that I can always remain quiet. I can't always avoid wanting to respond, wanting to continue the conflict; but I can back off, and that's more than half the battle. Backing off, or averting our attention, may be the closest thing to peace when first attempted.

It seems our best teachers are no doubt the ones we love the most and also the ones who get under our skin most often. Some would say our meeting was not accidental; our lessons aren't, either. Turning a great teacher into our most loved and intimate friend is what this journey is all about, perhaps. That seems sensible to me, anyway. How about to you?

◆

Every day someone who crosses our path cries out to be controlled or argued with or judged. Consider them God-sent. They are our teachers, one and all.

THE REASON DETACHMENT IS REWARDING IS THAT IT GIVES us so much relief. It allows us to thoroughly relax our bodies and our minds. It makes us feel reborn. And it gives us extra time to play for a change, to plant flowers perhaps, or read books, reconnect with old or new friends, take up painting or weaving or birding. It's amazing how much free time we have when we remove our attention from the many people and situations that didn't cotton to having our attention anyway.

But what does detachment reveal to us? Possibly that is an even more interesting consideration. What I have discovered is that detachment reveals we can live in concert with others, but we don't have to be in charge of each other or beholden to each other or controlled by each others' actions, opinions, wishes, or judgments. Detachment has revealed to me that I am far stronger than I ever thought, more resilient, courageous, creative, independent, and focused. My sense of self has soared since beginning the practice of detachment, and I know that I have no special powers. What has been true for me will certainly be true for anyone who applies the same effort I have applied.

I don't want to suggest that making a change of any kind is simple. Committing to the practice of detachment is a big change for most of us. But making any change incrementally is a good beginning. This will work with detachment, one opportunity at a time.

✦

To begin with, I detach in the little ways that matter. In that way we can see what's in store for us in the days ahead. We can begin today and notice how much better we feel.

Making the decision to detach from a loved one may well be the most important, as well as the kindest, gift we can give ourselves. Ever.

MOST OF US ARE QUITE AWARE WHEN WE ARE BEING LOVING to others and when we are withholding that love. We can feel it throughout our bodies. But are we as conscious of that expression of love toward ourselves? Perhaps not. And yet, with every breath we take, we are offering a whisper of self-love, or not, within the folds of that which we are expressing to others. There really is no separation between us and others. Initially this idea may not resonate with us, but it's nonetheless true.

I lived in a mindset of "us and them" for much of my life. Our culture seems to breed this idea in us, particularly when we consider the advertising that bombards us. Never are we encouraged to see others as fellow travelers who are the mirrors we need in order to better understand ourselves. But we can choose to see in them who we are and then when we offer compassion or acceptance or the gift of understanding *with detachment*, we are "gifting" ourselves as well. What we give, we also receive. The circle is made complete, with or without our awareness.

Seeing detachment as a gift may seem unusual to you. At the most superficial level, detachment seems like we are cutting ourselves off from others. But this is not what detachment means. It means to release another to be whoever is calling him from within. Preventing someone from hearing their own inner voice means we won't hear ours, either. Detachment releases both of us and that's the primary reason to value it.

✦

Choose one person today and practice detaching from whatever they are doing, if only for a few minutes. See how it feels. Take time to write about the feelings, too. This may well encourage you to try it again tomorrow.

Detachment is a swift and sure way
of expressing unconditional love.

127

DETACHMENT MAY NOT SEEM LIKE LOVE, BUT IT IS. BEING too involved in someone else's life, whether for an hour, a day, or a lifetime, means we are loving ourselves far less than we deserve and not showing others the kind of respect they deserve. We are not crossing one another's path to be in charge of them, but to complement them. The journey is intentional; what we learn is by design. What we are being invited to teach is by design as well. One of the primary lessons for all of us is to respect the natural boundaries between us. This we do by detaching from the emotions, the behaviors, and the opinions of others. Hopefully, our example will serve to show them how it's done, too.

Staying "on our side of the street" isn't as hard as it first appears to be, but until we experience the behavior, we can't know the relief it offers. From our shoulders down to our toes we actually realize a visceral freedom when we turn away from those affairs of others that are not ours to manage. There is no way of convincing someone how this feels, but it must be tried to be appreciated and then sought again for its own reward.

Detachment, as an expression of unconditional love, is easier than we first might imagine. Remaining quiet when we want to speak is a good beginning. Offering a silent prayer rather than a suggestion is another. Removing ourself from the setting entirely is also an obvious way to detach. But emotions may still be ensnared. Acting as if they aren't is a great practice until the real thing comes along. But it will take time. Patience is a virtue.

◆

Our greatest gift to someone else is unconditional love.
We all crave it; we all deserve it. Most of us have not
experienced it very often. Let's commit to breaking this cycle
now. Detachment is one of the ways.

Learning to detach is a process. It
moves faster for some than for others.
But the pace is not important.

HOW QUICKLY WE LEARN TO DETACH FROM EITHER THE
chaos or the mean-spiritedness present in the lives of others
isn't nearly as important as the commitment we make to doing
it. I have suggested before that it's the incremental efforts that
make the most difference. One quiet prayer, one passage of time
without a comment, one experience of walking away from a
potential conflict all add up to growth, the kind that convinces
us of the benefit of this new way of seeing life.

Change seldom happens quickly. The totally unexpected moment of full spiritual enlightenment is experienced by very few.
Tiny examples, generally perceived in retrospect, are what show
us change has occurred. The same is true with detachment. We
won't even notice initially that we have changed because it's so
subtle. But then, we see. We see that we are no longer tied to the
whims of others. We are no longer tied to the attacks of others.
Or the dismissals, the grunts, or the frowns of others. We will
suddenly see that God has helped us do what we had not before
been able to do for ourselves.

◆

The fact that we want to change is what's important. How
quickly that change happens rests with God. Our part is to
make the effort, daily.

Seeing God within our friends will help us
to let them live their own lives without our
control. Detachment can come in many ways.

129

SEEING GOD IN OTHERS IS CERTAINLY ONE WAY OF GETTING free of the need to control them. We all have our partnerships, and although we partner up with one another as spouses, lovers, and friends, our primary partnership is always with God. That's the One we can count on for guidance and for constant approval and acceptance. Getting any of these gifts from others can happen, but we can't count on that with any certainty. In other words, letting others be *in* our lives but not *of* our lives is how we truly live detached and joyful lives.

I have said before that an easy way to detach is simply to walk away quietly, rather than to be engaged in an argument that is escalating. It's also easy to simply smile and say, "Perhaps," rather than taking a discussion any further. But the easiest way to detach, for some, is to seek the face of Christ in one's friend. When this was first suggested to me, I scoffed. I had only ever seen His face in a picture. I am not sure even today that I really see His face in another, but I do see a light and I do feel compelled to let things be, regardless of the chaos. It's a change in perspective, and some call that a miracle. I will settle for the feeling I get, whatever it's called.

Experiencing detachment in multiple ways is worth the effort. What works well for one may not work as well for someone else. But I have yet to meet a person who was not able to detach when they really wanted freedom.

✦

If freedom from the pain of others' lives is what you seek, you have come to the right place. Any suggestion throughout this book will help you on your way. Willingness and tiny attempts are all it takes. God will help with the rest.

# 130
### Detachment is a tool that can be practiced with and by everyone.

NO ONE IS IMMUNE FROM THE EFFECTS OF DETACHMENT. When we are learning to detach from the behavior of those we love, we get moments of relief between spells of doubt that what we are doing is the right thing. When we can see that others are detaching from us and our chaotic thinking, it actually helps us slow down. When we can't engage others in our craziness, it begins to be diffused.

Everyone benefits from the practice of detachment. It could probably be proven that one's health is improved as the result of detachment too. Taking a deep breath is good for all our cells and that's the first step of detachment, after all. And when our friends and loved ones can see that we are no longer trapped by their chaos, they quiet down too. And if the struggle continues, we have many more steps we can take.

I have considered how valuable this tool could be if applied to world powers. Unfortunately, too many leaders feel that walking away is the coward's way. Of course we might see that as a show of strength too, one that implies that it's okay for you to have your opinion. I'll keep mine. And we will peacefully coexist. People, individually, do it all the time. Just maybe it's time to envision this on a broader scale and see what the results could be.

✦

Surrendering to the practice of detachment is a healthy choice for every one. Our example might be the only example another person is privy to today. Let's not disappoint them.

# pause *and* reflect

One moment at a time—that's all we have. And that's all the
time we need to detach.

Being accountable for ourselves only is the best assurance of
living detachment.

Learning to detach from our most difficult companions pays
huge dividends.

Detachment may not look like unconditional love, but it is.

Making someone a hostage makes us a hostage, too.

This is an excellent time to step back and honestly inventory your behavior in regard to others. Are you giving
them the space they need to grow? Are you allowing
yourself the independence you need to grow? Where can
you see evidence of this? Make a journal entry so you have
it to turn to on those days when you get overly involved
in the affairs of others.

What's the most valuable payoff you have experienced
from the practice of detachment? Is there a friend who
needs to hear your story of growth? Watch for the opportunity to share it today.

Detaching from our companions
does not mean discounting them,
dismissing them, or rejecting them.

KEEPING OUR FOCUS ON OUR OWN LIVES IN NO WAY
means we don't care about other people. Letting others be free
of our focus is actually a gift to them. As a youngster, I seldom
averted my eyes from others' activities. I was obsessed with wondering what they were thinking about and if it related to me.
Was I "okay?" Were they mad at me? Were they going to rep-
rimand me or reject me? This obsession didn't leave me until a
few years after finding Al-Anon. The miracle is that it did leave.

I know that what happened for me can happen for anyone.
I am certainly not special. What I did to help the process—and
I learned this in the Twelve Step rooms—was to replace my
thoughts of others with a vision of my Higher Power. I asked
God for help many times a day to give me peace of mind and
a different focus. And I asked to be more conscious of serving
others, rather than always looking to be served.

When others detach from us, it doesn't mean that they don't
love us. They are allowing us to grow. This valuable tool works
well in the hands of all of us. We all grow in ways that are important to the entire human community when we free people
to be who they have been born to be. Holding on keeps all of
us stuck. Letting go frees everyone.

✦

No one wants to be rejected or to feel dismissed. We all
want to know we matter. But being the center of someone's
life doesn't mean love. It may mean dependence, and that
holds everyone hostage.

USING "KEEP IT SIMPLE" AS A MANTRA THROUGHOUT THE day can offer so much relief. It's a nice reminder that we are not the managers of the world. We are not the managers of others' lives. Some even say that our own life is none of our business, either. Letting each and every life be God's business is a choice we can make. It's a wise choice, in fact. Our shoulders relax, our breathing slows down, and our mind gets quiet when we decide to just "keep it simple" and stop doing that which we need not do.

Being able to say, "Keep it simple" over and over is similar to repeating the Serenity Prayer. It fills our mind with a softness that invites us to change our focus from where it was. The first time I saw the wall poster with the words "keep it simple," I couldn't fathom what it actually meant and why it would be hanging on a recovery room wall. What did it have to do with my situation? And what was the "it" that it referred to? Finally, I heard others share, using the phrase in ways that showed me how they kept their focus on themselves and away from others' business. I could see how much better they felt than I was feeling. And I wanted what they had.

Seeing others in action is what teaches all of us that we can act differently, too. Attraction rather than promotion is one of the principles of Twelve Step recovery, and I was definitely attracted to the peace and well-being that others had. Offering that to others, now, keeps me coming back.

✦

Keeping it simple makes every day easier, more productive, and quiet. Being an example of "keeping it simple" keeps us away from managing those things that are not ours to manage. This may be our most important contribution today.

DETACHING FROM THE ACTIVITIES OF OTHERS MAY BE AN
exercise of will, initially. In an almost mindless way, some of us
simply hang on to those people in our midst, assuming they
need our attention, our judgment, and our input on every detail
of their lives.

Or perhaps we hang on because we aren't sure who *we* are if
they aren't present. This was my struggle for decades. I needed
another's acknowledgment to know that I mattered. I feel embarrassed, at times, to look back to those days; then I remember
that my struggle is why I can help others who have been sent
my way that are struggling now in the same way. Everything we
learn is recyclable. And this is as it should be.

Releasing ourselves from the companions we intentionally
walk among does not mean we are relinquishing the friendships,
the learning opportunities, or the growth. It only means we are
allowing the kind of growth that needs to happen for all of us
to unfold when the timing is right. Our attachments to others
are not healthy, for any of us. And others aren't ever present for
that reason. Let's not forget that.

◆

The work you and I have to do here may relate to those we
walk with, but there will always be a line between my work
and yours. Seeking to see the line is the best lesson of all on
many days.

Perfecting detachment is a lifelong
journey. But prayer will help.

134

I HAVE OFTEN PONDERED WHAT IT MIGHT FEEL LIKE TO have perfected a skill like detachment on a first attempt. Or even on the one-hundredth attempt. And I have concluded that had that been my story, I might have quit showing up at the Twelve Step meetings where I was learning about this valuable skill. And it's in *those* meetings that real magic occurs. It's in those meetings that hearts and minds and souls connect and all of us have a chance to change in ways that were unimaginable before. It's in those meetings that God always makes an appearance.

Some days I have to pinch myself to realize that the life I have been blessed with is real. My life had been so far from what it has become that one explanation is all that fits: God was *always* doing for me what I could not do for myself, and didn't even want to do for myself. I had charted a course that was self-centered, codependent in every way, and riddled with alcohol and drug escapades. And yet, I am here. Prayer played a major role (during that troubled time, other people's prayers) in getting me where I am and still does.

I did used to think that those who relied on prayer were weak. Now I know that my strength for handling any situation comes from the God of my understanding. Nothing I used to believe rings true anymore.

✦

Learning to detach is like breathing. Enjoy the process. It's what being alive is all about. It's why the other people are in your life. There's no escaping the opportunities. But be grateful. Some of them are fleeting.

## 135 Detaching from others doesn't preclude joining with them in a healthy way on occasion.

DETACHING FROM OTHERS DOES NOT MEAN DENYING THEIR presence. It's not a negative action at all. It's definitely not shunning those people who are in our lives. It's much more akin to living in a positive place with others and keeping one's focus where it really belongs: on ourselves. We never have to walk away and stay away from others unless we choose to do so. Detachment allows us to be friends, lovers, and companions. It's simply a healthy way to be with all three groups.

The deeper purpose for sharing this journey with loved ones is the inner growth we experience when we intimately join with the minds and hearts of others. But the idea of joining with others is not an invitation to try to control what someone else might think or do. Joining *with* is not the opposite of detaching *from*. They are complementary. We can be lovingly detached in a way that supports being lovingly joined. In fact, that's the real goal, and it's a daily practice for most of us. The good news is that every little success we have makes it easier to apply the process the next day.

To lovingly detach means I love you unconditionally and trust you to make the next right decision. To lovingly join means I honor the steps you need to take and will accompany you if that's your choice.

✦

What we are learning here takes time. We can't be discouraged. There is no rush; the opportunities will continue. And they will wait for us.

BEING ABLE TO EMOTIONALLY DETACH FROM CHAOS MIGHT be considered an art form. It certainly isn't an easy mind shift. It takes willingness, followed by determination, to be quiet in the midst of turmoil. And yet, no turmoil really has to capture us. We can observe it and move on. Perhaps we'll make some quiet judgments, but they don't have to be voiced, and we will find, in time, that even the quiet judgments fall away.

We can always adopt silence rather than agitation or interference or all-out battle. It's an interesting realization, I think. It's one that I fought accepting for far too many years, to my detriment and to the detriment of many of my relationships. I felt like I had to speak up, for myself and others. If not me, then who would do it?

There are so many quieter ways to live, aren't there? The quiet way is not a sign of fear or being intimidated or having a lack of interest. It's really a show of respect to ourselves and to others. Making the decision to choose the silent way of seeing today, in even one instance, is a good experiment. See how it feels. Not having to speak is quite exhilarating, actually. And making that a choice is even more pleasant.

◆

The way that choosing silence will make you feel will surprise you, I think. It does not make you feel powerless but empowered. A wise choice.

IT'S CERTAINLY POSSIBLE THAT SOMEONE READING THIS book already had the gift of letting others go from the time they became aware of those others all around them. But most of us had to develop the trait, which meant we had to first become willing to experience certain aspects of our life differently, to try new behavior, to strengthen a relationship with a Higher Power, for instance. Seeing ourselves always in relationship to others wasn't unusual, particularly as youngsters. But when the time came for us to separate, to feel whole while alone, fear was invoked and codependency reared its very ugly head.

If that's the struggle you are still having, you will be happy to know that there is a solution, the same solution that has been shared in so many of these essays. With your Higher Power's help, seek to see your many companions as the members of your own specific classroom, not as your hostages. We are here to learn. We all showed up for that purpose. But we can't learn unless we are willing to open our minds and see each other in a new way. Some refer to this as a shift in perspective, and then others call this shift a miracle. You will be transformed, either way.

◆

Making a different choice to see a companion as a teacher is quite a shift in how you perceive him or her. Take a moment to enjoy this idea and then apply it as soon as you can.

Asking a friend to witness our practice
of detachment is an interesting and
worthwhile opportunity—for both parties.

HAVING OTHERS "EXPERIENCE" OUR EFFORTS BY WATCHING
us when we attempt something as subtle as detachment is a rich
and rewarding activity. Their attention honors us. They can offer
feedback. They can seek to understand more about the process
of detachment: how it feels, what's to be gained, how to do it
themselves. We learn by doing and also by imitating those who
do. Detachment is one of those skills that seldom comes easy.

Even though detachment doesn't come easy, it will be realized
if it is your heart's desire. Nothing that's really of value is very
easy to accomplish, is it? Getting a college degree, for instance,
takes times, commitment, honest perseverance, and most of all,
humility. Being able to detach is a very humbling experience,
too. We will fail, many times. But the serious among us will
try again and again. The number of times we fall is not so very
important. What's important is the number of times we get up
and try again.

Inviting a friend in our life to hold out hope for us as we
work on developing detachment may well be all the encour-
agement we need. And it's a gift to that person, as well. Helping
others insures that we will get back that which we need, too.
What goes around, comes around, as they say.

◆

Setting the goal of detaching from a situation or person
today, and inviting a friend to take note of our efforts, is a
great exercise. Make a plan for this before the day begins.

I CAN'T THINK OF A SINGLE SKILL THAT IS MASTERED AFTER only one attempt. Learning to walk and tie shoes and brush teeth take many attempts before success is obvious. And with so many of these skills, we don't expect perfection immediately. Although we may want to be good golfers after only a few rounds or good tennis players after just a few sets, we don't honestly think it's possible. We do know that gradual progress is much more the norm.

Detachment falls into the same category. We have to do it over and over in order to get the feel of what it even means. It's not a natural response to the people in our lives. We were born caretakers, hoping that this was reciprocal: we hoped that whatever we gave, we would also receive in return. But giving in order to get is not the way that giving was designed to work.

Detachment is about release—the release of all those other people we have been watching too closely, the release of our own emotions from having them too tightly tied to the behavior of others. Detachment can only happen one moment at a time. It's not a "one time only" solution that solves all problems. Every encounter with every person offers another opportunity to detach. With enough practice, we will get good at it. We got good at tying our shoes, didn't we?

+

Some believe that skills which take practice are more valued. If so, detachment will become one of our most prized skills. I know it has changed my life.

Detachment promises peace of mind.
Does this make it God's will?

140

WE CAN'T BE CERTAIN THAT DETACHMENT IS GOD'S WILL, but I do think it's safe to say that God wills peaceful minds for all of us. I know that having more peace in my life as the result of minding fewer people's business feels wonderful. Living this way makes me happier, and I have no doubt that it makes the significant people in my life happier, too. But it takes a daily commitment to turn away when we'd rather get into the thick of someone else's life. To reap the benefit of detachment, there is only one choice for us to make, however.

Trying to determine whether or not detachment is God's will for any one of us is irrelevant. I have come to believe that His will is the expression of love, and in my life there is no greater expression of love than to let my friends, my husband, and my colleagues take control of their own lives. This doesn't have to mean that I don't care what they do. I do care, but I don't need to sound the alarm when I think they are making a wrong choice or an irresponsible decision. When asked, share. Otherwise, mum's the word.

This may be a new way of seeing life for many who are sharing these meditations. I wasn't born believing in the value of detachment. When first introduced to the term, I was baffled. Now it's the most important skill I attempt to practice on a daily basis. It is what assures me of having peace of mind. Nothing else works.

◆

Having a peaceful mind is such a blessing. If this isn't "where you live" very often, give detachment from the affairs of others a try. You won't regret it.

# pause *and* reflect

There is no timeline in learning how to detach. We have all
the time we need. But the more quickly we begin the
practice, the more peaceful our lives will be.
Progress, not perfection, is the outcome we should seek.
Dismissing or discounting someone is definitely not
detachment.
Praying for the willingness to let others have their own
journeys is the first step to letting go of them.
When in doubt about how to respond in any situation,
choose silence for sixty seconds at least.

We uncover so many unexpected opportunities in our
dealings with others. Observing yourself in your encounters will teach you a great deal about yourself. Let today
be the day to truly witness yourself in action. Make brief
notes of what you see as quickly as possible. The idea is
to learn who we are so that we can change who we are.
Can you see areas in your life that you want to change?

Do you see the stumbling blocks to making those
changes? What are they and how can you make them
work for you rather than against you?

Our relationships with others have many charac-teristics. We may allow for differences in our viewpoints with some but not with others. We may more easily allow for more freedom to act in ways counter to our own way of thinking with some, too. With a few, perhaps, we hold the reins tightly, to no one's advantage. The choices we have are myriad; some are more insightful and helpful than others to everyone present. Others are exasperating or stifling.

When we are selecting among the many choices to find the one most beneficial to our situation, we have to sit back and consider the consequences. There will be some, there always are. But consequences are not always negative. One of the consequences of the practice of detachment is a quieter mind, and that's good. Another consequence is the freedom our family members feel to be themselves. In the process, we feel the rush of relief run through our bodies, too. Again, that's a good consequence. Just knowing that we are not responsible for others' failures is freeing. Everyone is given power over their own actions when we practice detachment. Allowing others to be accountable for themselves is one of the best gifts we can ever give them.

◆

Preparing ourselves for this day ahead invites us to pause and seek God's will. We will be guided regarding what to do, and if we can't hear the message, let's make sure our choices are beneficial to all.

WANTING TO CRITICIZE OTHERS SEEMS NATURAL, AS THOUGH
it is part of the human condition. It's not. We have nearly made
it so, but there are those who don't criticize others. My aunt
Helen was one of them. Never did she speak ill of others. It was
a marvelous, almost mystical quality. How did she do it? we all
wondered. It wasn't because her life was easy. On the contrary,
she was widowed very young and had six children to raise right
after the second world war. She did it without complaint and
without holding others hostage with her criticism or her control. She lived her life with God as her primary partner after Leo
was gone, and she knew peace.

Just having known Aunt Helen gives me the inspiration to
believe that I too can give up criticism, that I too can know
peace. Letting others be all that they need or want to be, without
my input, is the easiest way to experience it. But I have to make
detachment from all of them my primary mode of operation on
a daily basis. On those days when I do, I am comfortably peaceful. I feel more rested, more certain that I am living God's will.
And on those days that I let another's affairs become mine, I am
in chaos. The insanity of letting the affairs of others become ours
debilitates us. Most of us are works in progress.

✦

Doing anything for one day is possible. Giving up criticism is
a great choice for this experiment. It's a way of succeeding
at two skills: detachment and nonjudgment.

WHY, YOU MIGHT ASK, DOES DETACHMENT REQUIRE A
new way of thinking? Certainly, I am not here to suggest that
everyone alive needs a new way of thinking. But it's my guess,
since you were prompted to pick up this book, that detachment
either has some appeal for you, has mystified you in the past, has
defeated you previously, or has simply called out to you because
of the turmoil in current relationships. No matter what the reason, detachment, as a means of moving through the day in all
relationships, is guaranteed to reflect new thinking.

Very few of us knew, without some prompting, that we
should consider a new way of thinking. We may have felt ennui
or confusion or even major disappointment as the result of the
behavior of others. But this didn't necessarily inform us that we
needed to consider anything differently in our lives—that is,
until we simply couldn't find peace in any experience. Then the
message began to seep in: we needed to try a different approach.

This new way of thinking isn't mysterious, really. It's not
complicated. It's quiet. It's easily chosen but not always easily
practiced. But, as I said before, any new skill takes time, and this
reversal of our thinking—what is quite completely a reversal in
thinking for the typical codependent as a matter of fact—takes
time. Beginning with the reminder, "Keep a quiet mind and
say nothing," we will develop the skill we need. It's really rather
pleasant once you get the hang of it.

✦

**The old way of thinking was to hang on tight. Letting go is a
big departure. It's also life giving in such a rich way.**

Detachment implies giving up control.

WANTING TO CONTROL SOME ASPECT, EVEN SOME TINY little detail, of someone else's life is such a common thread in the lives of most of us. We just can't let go of control, or the illusion of it, and *it is an illusion* to think we can control someone else. Even the parent who withholds a bike or an allowance or a night out with friends can't really be sure that the child's behavior will change. For a day, perhaps, but for more? Not likely. Control is simply a fallacy. Our attempts to control other people will be no more successful than holding back the rain.

If we really could control others, our burdens would be heavy. Our work would never, ever, be finished. Why then do we think we want the power to control others? For years I pondered this. I think it's because we think that if others do as we ask, it's a sign of love, and love is what we fear losing most of all. When others give in to our way of thinking, it's because they love us unconditionally—or so we tell ourselves. Only then can we rest and feel secure.

The fallacy of this runs so deep. Others doing our will has nothing to do with love. They simply may be tired of the battle. How much more serene our lives would be if we gave up the battle too. Deciding to detach is our invitation to live lives of ease. Someone else may not give up the battle, but let's do it ourselves.

◆

To give up control is a peaceful decision. Everyone is blessed by it. But no one more than you.

A PARENT AT ONE OF MY MEETINGS FELT CERTAIN THAT IF she let her son go, he'd die. We tried to explain by sharing our own experience, strength, and hope that indeed, that might be the case, but that holding on would not prevent it, either. To detach one's emotions, to give up the attempt to control, makes one feel so vulnerable, so naked to chance, so irresponsible when a loved one is teetering on the edge. Detachment is not for the faint of heart.

Detaching is all that may save our loved ones, however. How does this work? If others are expecting us to pick up the many little pieces of a broken life, again and again, without apply= ing any effort themselves, we will be undermining them to the point of annihilation. It won't come quickly, but it will come. Our fear, in reality, could well be the nail in their coffin. Not a pleasant realization. The lament that "All I wanted to do was save him" is heard repeatedly at the funerals of loved ones. But finally, our best effort is to detach and allow our loved ones to seek their own path, fulfill their own journey, with the help of their own Higher Power. We are not that Power. Their choices are not ours to make or to even approve.

When our focus is on someone else, we need to refocus. Let= ting others find their own way is the most likely way that they will find a life worth living.

◆

We can practice refocusing as many times as is necessary today. It's a good practice too. It will make tomorrow's attempts even easier.

## 146 Unconditional love can be packaged in many ways. Detachment may not seem like one of them, but it is.

BEFORE I SOUGHT HELP FOR MY CODEPENDENCY, I WANTED a show of affection from everyone. I wanted favorable attention to prove others had seen me and approved of my presence. I thought my self-worth depended on it. But I was disappointed again and again. The attention often wasn't forthcoming. The affection was fleeting. My self-worth plummeted, but I didn't give up. I was adamant about getting others to focus specifically on me, but seldom were my pleas honored. How grateful I am now that my intention wasn't realized.

Perhaps that seems like an odd statement, but I have learned the value of discovering my own inner worth through my relationship to my Higher Power. And I believe that's what your primary relationship should look like, too. The best gift that others gave to me was the gift to let me find my own way. Now the best gift I can give to others is to let them do the same.

It's not a gift many of us appreciate when we first receive it. We can easily misinterpret it. But giving to our loved ones their lives to live, however they choose, is good for them and for us. It shows respect. It's a way of saying, "You are worth so much more than what I can give you." It takes a while for this to sink in, but it will. And then everything will be less difficult, for both parties. And our love will be stronger than ever.

◆

The love we give others should never have strings attached. Honoring the independence of a loved one is love, even when their choices worry us.

Saying "I can choose peace instead of this"
is one way of embracing detachment.

147

QUIETLY REFUSING TO GET TRAPPED IN THE BUSINESS OF others is a wise decision, one that will allow us to remain friends with them, if that's our choice. So seldom do our friends or family members really want us to interfere. They may want to know what we would do if we were in their shoes, and delicately, we might answer that question. But usually it is far better to simply say, "My own experience has taught me . . . ," and then to elaborate.

There will be many opportunities everyday to murmur, "I can choose peace instead of this," and it's effective every time we use it. Every time! It prompts us to turn away, letting the turmoil go on without us. Even when it's an argument we'd love to enter, we can opt to let it pass and to choose peace instead. This is one of the most exhilarating principles I have adopted in more than thirty-five years on a Twelve Step recovery path.

Taking a stand for peace in tiny arguments as well as in family chaos is adding to the peace that's being registered around the world. That has made this choice even more appealing to me. Many times a day I get to practice sending forth a breath of peace that will be felt by others, and as more of us do this, I think a shift in the universe will finally occur.

✦

Consciously choosing to be peaceful isn't always easy. In fact, inside we might feel agitated, at first. But acting as if you feel peace is a beginning. Give it a try today. Your attempt will be felt far and wide.

THE OPTION TO NOT REACT, PARTICULARLY WITH CERTAIN people, is almost impossible to choose. It's as though we are caught in a magnetic field with them, and before we know what's hit us, we have spouted off. Then the fireworks begin. But must they?

That's the point of this meditation—of this entire book, in fact. We can begin the practice of detachment anytime, with any person. The unfriendly cashier at the grocery store doesn't have to get under our skin. The driver behind us who insists on honking when we can't move forward can be "blessed" and let go, rather than allowing him rent=free space in our minds. Our spouses or children need not receive our wrath, ever. The choice to be quiet, to not react regardless of the seduction to do so, feels good, very good. And the more this becomes our practice, the less others will ever bother us.

I have heard it said that our best teachers are those people who cause us the most unease. I used to think that if I simply found a new relationship partner, my problems would be solved. Now I am grateful to be able to appreciate all that I have learned from all my difficult relationships. But what has made this pos= sible is the practice of detachment, day in and day out.

✦

Before many breaths have been taken, an opportunity
to detach will occur today. Remember that it's a decision
that gets made by hundreds of millions of people every day.
Why not add your voice to this group?

DETACHMENT SOUNDS LIKE DISAVOWAL, I KNOW. BUT IT'S nothing like that. It took me a while to decipher the real meaning of detachment; so if that's your struggle right now, you're in good company. Anyone who has chosen to read this book most likely has been more comfortable attaching to others, rather than trying to detach from them. Our security, or I should say *my* security, rested with having a significant partner committed to me. If he turned away from me or lost interest permanently, I was devastated.

Whether or not my many relationship partners were just practicing detachment or rejecting me outright, I'll never know. I do know now, however, that whatever someone else does need not define me. I also know now that I can join with others in a healthy, spiritual way and not be attached to them.

Detaching means letting our own inner voice decide for us what to think and do, rather than letting the "outer voice" of someone else decide. It's not very complicated to understand, really, but initially it's fairly complicated to execute. It's such a joy to know that we can join with people on this journey and not feel controlled by them. Their voices do not determine our actions, our value, or our mindset. That's our purview, and only ours.

✦

We are not denying the importance of others to our lives when we detach from them. We are only establishing the importance of our own lives.

Detachment from others is the
opposite of being obsessed.

It's not just people we get obsessed with. Alcohol, food, drugs, chocolate, to name just a few, are high on the list of things that people become obsessed with. But getting free of the obsession with certain people often helps to alleviate our obsession with other substances. Our concern here, however, is with people.

How do we get free of the need to control them? Why must we see their behavior as a reflection on us? Why must they change in order for us to feel adequate? The answer to all these questions is the same, really. Our security, once and for all, lies with no one but God and our relationship with Him. And we need not be obsessed with that relationship for it to give us peace. We need do little more than seek to know God better for the grace to come.

Obsession with anyone or anything kills one's spirit. Nothing else can get our attention when we are in the throes of obses-sion. We can't know the joys that are passing by if the image or the presence of someone else has dominated our thinking and our behavior. So much is being offered to us every day. Too much is being missed if we aren't eagerly opening our minds every minute in anticipation of the new information, the people, and the spiritual messages that are always there.

✦

Obsession doesn't feel good. It's noisy. It's never peaceful and never fruitful. But there is another choice. Today can be the day to give the other choice a royal try.

# pause *and* reflect

Detachment is a choice.
Unconditional love is a choice.
Giving up control is a choice.
Being afraid is a choice.
Choosing to be peaceful is a choice.
Choosing to act, rather than react, is a choice.
Trusting our companions to live their own lives is a choice.

Every good thing in our lives is the outgrowth of making good choices. What good choices have you made lately? Use your journal to respond to these questions.
Where have these choices led you?

What doors have opened, or closed, because of these choices?

What do you most want to change about your life to=day? Make a plan, here and now, and share it with at least one other person to make yourself more accountable.

FEW OF US WANT TO BE WATCHED. WE MAY WANT TO BE the object of someone's loving attention, but that's not the same as being spied on. We don't want it and neither do the partners we may currently be spying on. But we get into the habit of spying when we are uncertain of ourselves and even more uncertain of the activities of our loved ones. When we get caught in this cycle, it's time to stand back, remind ourselves who our Higher Power is, remind ourselves who our loved one's Higher Power is, and then go on about our own lives, lovingly detached.

The tension we so often feel around others, regardless of who they are, is generally the result of overinvolvement in their lives. We want to control their decisions so that they fit our needs; maybe we want to protect them from dangers that may well be necessary to their journey; or we want to create outcomes that favor our dreams. The list goes on, but the intent is the same.

When we are caught in this web of control, illusory though it may be, we quickly feel exhausted from the tension it causes in our shoulders, our foreheads, and throughout our bodies. There is only one way to find release: to detach, from them, their plans, their journeys, our own dreams of what their journeys should be. And this we can do. With practice we can even do it well.

◆

There is no better time or day to begin this practice. Your tension will quickly leave you. When it returns, you will know why. And you will know the solution.

Detaching from our family members allows
them to grow in ways unique to them.

152

DETACHING FROM MEMBERS OF ONE'S FAMILY CERTAINLY
does not imply a lack of love. On the contrary, it generally means
a measure of honest affection. It is a demonstration of trust that
the loved one will listen to his or her Higher Power and make
the decisions that are right for their own path. None of us can
hear the Higher Power of another. Therefore, we can't know
what's truly best for someone else. We can know what *we think*
is best, but that generally reflects our own specific desire for
their life.

If we could only remember what we have gleaned from the
spiritual wisdom of myriad others: that every one of us has a
uniquely chosen path, with a predetermined destination and a
host of encounters that have been preplanned. This means, without contradiction, that our loved ones must be left alone to live
out their own plans. They don't need our input. They need our
prayers, perhaps; our hopes for them when they are faltering; our
words of experience coupled with our strength, if sought, and
only if sought. But they do not need our interference.

Letting our loved ones grow, as they must, will be the most
treasured of all the gifts we can bestow on them. It may well be
the hardest one for us to part with, but it will be the best gift we
can give both them and ourselves.

◆

> Letting others go to make their own way is not easy, but
> that's what we have all come here to do. We can help
> each other by detaching. There is no better time than
> now to begin.

NOT EVERYONE SEEKS TO BE FULLY ACCOUNTABLE FOR
his or her life. In fact, many don't. They are very willing to let
others do for them what they really need to do for themselves,
and when they succeed in getting this help, they are cheating
themselves and the helper too.

I am not suggesting that we never help one another. It's one
of the ways we join our spirits. But we all recognize those times
when we should let go and let our friend or partner solve his or
her own problem, because problems are related to the lessons we
have all come here to master. Serving as the supporting "angel"
in another person's life is not the same as being the servant who
does their work.

Being responsible to ourselves is key to our having real joy on
a daily basis. This is true for those we walk with, too. We commonly take on another's tasks because we want them to like us
even more, thinking this will increase our joy. Alas, the reverse
generally happens in time. We simply must honor the responsi-
bilities of others and handle only our own. Every meditation in
this small book is showing you how. It's a simple decision, really.
It's only the follow=through that requires practice.

✦

Knowing there is a tool that can help every one of us be
more responsible is a good thing. Using this tool must
become habitual, however. Today is a good day to give it a
try. There will be opportunities, there always are.

Our willingness to detach from
our loved ones demonstrates to
them that we trust them.

154

THE VALUE OF TRUST CAN'T BE OVERSTATED. TRUSTING OUR
Higher Power to answer our prayers, listen to our hopes, and
grant those desires that are right for us relieves us of the constant
worry that what we need will not be forthcoming. Indeed, what
we *need* is guaranteed. What we want may not be right for us at
this time, however. The same is true for others. That's why we
must let them do their own praying, seeking the help they need
from God as they understand Him. We are not in their service.
We can hold hope for them, but that's the extent of our work.

I have heard many at Twelve Step meetings say they tell loved
ones, "I know you will handle this and make the right decision. I
have faith in you." In this way, they remove themselves from the
equation and allow the other person the dignity to grow. Doing
for others what they need to be doing stunts their growth. This
will come back to haunt us in time, because everyone instinctively knows when we have interfered.

Trust is a gift we give ourselves and others. So is detachment.
They go hand in hand. One strengthens the other, and both create a shift in our perception of life that's miraculous.

◆

It's not easy to detach the first few times we try it. We fear
that our loved ones will fail or that they want our control. In
time we will learn the value of letting them go. And the gift
will be immeasurable to all of us.

BEING TOLD THAT I NEEDED TO DISCERN GOD'S WILL when I first entered the rooms of recovery more than baffled me. I had never even considered the concept of *God's will* before. I am quite certain I had never heard anyone talk about God's will. Then a friend explained it like this: God is Love; Will is Thought; therefore God's will is loving thought. That I could resonate with. He next said, "Your job is to love others, and God will do the rest."

I was relieved to know there was a directive for how to live my life. But I soon discovered that having a "rule book" didn't mean I could really do what it suggested. I listened to the others I gathered with on a regular basis, though, and could see that what they often did was nothing, rather than trying to do something that wasn't really part of their assignment.

I couldn't understand, initially, how doing nothing might be construed as loving, but in time I was blessed with clarity. My overinvolvement helped no one. Practicing the art of doing nothing began to make a lot of sense. Detachment thus became my goal every day. It is never an unloving act. It's a demonstration of trust and confidence and healthy independence. It's one of the most honorable ways to pay homage to a loved one.

✦

Detaching from our loved ones is allowing them to go to the God of their understanding for the solutions they need. Every one of us hears God in our own way. And this is, in fact, God's will.

Detachment might first begin with
a vision of doing it successfully.

156

BEING ABLE TO "SEE" OURSELVES SUCCEEDING AT SOME-
thing is often the first step to meeting with the success we long
for. Olympic athletes occasionally practice by envisioning their
runs prior to the day of the event. I have had direct experience with this too when preparing for a major oral exam. The
practice, even though only in the mind, offers a sense of having
been there already. It's quite effective. Psychologists agree. Why,
then, wouldn't the concept apply to the exercise of detachment?

If you are in a relationship that you struggle with, one that
seems to scream for your overinvolvement, take a few moments
every morning and sit quietly in deep silence with eyes closed,
envisioning being able to walk away when the temptation to
speak is strong. See yourself smiling within, calmly breathing,
and simply minding your own business. Notice how much more
peaceful you feel. Savor that feeling. Sit with it a while.

Now, when the opportunity to react to what someone is
saying or doing presents itself, as it will, draw on the experience
that your earlier vision gave you. You don't have to get sucked
into someone else's drama. The freedom you will experience
just might become the elixir you had been seeking through the
power of control.

✦

Sit quietly for a moment upon awakening and visualize who
you want to be for the day. That will become a practice that
can change your life considerably.

**Surrendering control is another way to think of detachment.**

To some, the term *surrender* may seem like defeat. It does mean "to give in." But when we are using it in the context of relationships with significant people in our lives, surrendering means letting them have their own beliefs rather than insisting they adopt ours. It's not a term of defeat but one of acceptance: accepting others as they are rather than as we might prefer them to be.

Detachment, when thought of as acceptance, offers a different slant to the process. For some, thinking of detachment as acceptance will make it more palatable. Letting others be who they are in every situation is a gift beyond measure to them and to us. Every time we surrender to a situation with someone else, we give ourselves freedom from the anxiety that trying to control them engenders in us. We generally don't recognize the price we are paying in trying to control others until we have quit paying it. Then the relief comes over us and we finally know peace.

The decision to accept others exactly as they are isn't made easily, but once the die is cast, nothing about how we experience them or any situation remains the same. Our lives shift significantly when we practice acceptance.

◆

Surrendering isn't defeat, it's freedom. The practice is lifelong and rewarding, day after day.

The freedom to live our lives can't be accomplished unless we detach ourselves from the lives of others.

IF WE HAVE BEEN CODEPENDENTLY ATTACHED TO OTHERS who journey with us, we have not given ourselves, or them, the freedom to experience real growth. Being *with others* is natural; that's why they are present. But letting those others be the central focus of our own lives doesn't allow us to see what's standing before us that needs our attention.

There is a difference between joining with others for the shared experiences that are designed to complement our lives and not allowing ourselves the freedom to step away and do our own, very specific work. Detachment and joining with others are not mutually exclusive. To "join with" another is a loving, shared experience. Detachment is loving, too. It doesn't ever mean to push someone aside in a mean way. It simply means to "move aside," so each of us can do the work we are here to do.

Having specific work is good. That's why we are here. Let's remember that the same is true for our fellow travelers. We can show support for them, and should. We can hold out hope for them, and should. We can offer prayers for them, and should. The rest is up to them. And that's as it should be.

◆

We complicate our journey by being too focused on the path of someone else. There is another way. Let's seek it today.

## Detachment is a loving choice, one among many.

A MAN CAME INTO AN AL-ANON MEETING IN ANGUISH. He had practiced detaching, with love, and his son overdosed on drugs and died. The sadness in the room was palpable, as was the silence. In time, the voices of love and acceptance began to be heard, and the man's quivering shoulders relaxed. He heard from all of us that he was not the cause of the overdose. The disease was at fault, and his detaching from his son had been the right thing to do. His son's life was not his to control. Now he had to detach from the consequences of his son's actions, too.

Few acts of detachment have such a dramatic conclusion, but all acts of detachment allow for unknown consequences. Knowing that every "son" has a Higher Power, that every outcome is beyond our control, encourages us to make the right choice, the choice to detach regardless of what our fears might be.

No one said this was easy. I assure you, it's not, and it takes courage, daily practice, and the willingness to suspend our disbelief that we can't do it or that it won't work. We can and it will! I have seen it work in the lives of hundreds, perhaps thousands, of people, and it works in my life, too. Remembering that it is the loving choice, regardless of the outcome, makes it easier to select when the call to control is heard.

✦

Selecting the loving choice will help us through the day.
Think detach when the call to interfere is registering on
your mind.

Maintaining healthy boundaries is key
to good relationships. Knowing when
to detach is crucial to the process.

160

THERE WAS A TIME IN MY PAST THAT I COULD NOT HAVE
defined what *boundary* even meant in terms of my relationships.
I was enmeshed with my loved ones, and I liked it that way. My
security was defined by it. But then the royal rejection occurred.
I didn't know who I was without him. I didn't know what I
liked, what I thought, what to even hope for. I floundered and
tried to take hostages. Fortunately, my attempts were not very
successful. I had begun to surround myself with others who
were healthier than me, and they didn't want to be enmeshed.
They understood the importance of boundaries and thus my
education began.

I look back on that period with gratitude. I couldn't be where
I am now without the painful past I experienced. That I sought
enmeshment for so many years taught me so much that I am
now passing on to others. That's how it works. We learn and then
we give it away, just as it was given to us.

My insecurity pushed me to try to make hostages of the
people who showed an interest in me. Their security pushed me
away. It was a tough learning curve, but I began to appreciate
their detachment as offering me the freedom I needed but had
never claimed or understood. Now, that is what I try to demonstrate to others. The circle is complete.

◆

Having a healthy boundary doesn't mean not caring about
those who are close to us. It actually means caring enough
about them to let them live unencumbered by our control.

# pause *and* reflect

The power of the imagination can't be overstated.
Visualize yourself being lovingly detached first.
There is no race to the finish line. We are all works in progress.
Your assignments cannot be fulfilled if your attention is
   on someone else, rather than on the work you are here
   to perform.

Make a practice for the next few days of meditating every morning, holding in your mind a picture of yourself peacefully letting everyone move freely in his or her own life. At the end of the day, recount your experiences in your journal. Was there a change in how your day felt? If not, practice more earnestly. That change is guaranteed.

What was your specific assignment today? Could you glean what God was intending for you to learn? Give thanks to Him before you retire tonight for His constant patience.

We will have more opportunities to practice our "work" tomorrow.

GOD WILL ALWAYS DO FOR US WHAT WE CAN'T, BUT SHOULD, be doing. God will not help us with those things that aren't on our spiritual agenda, but He will be available, unfailingly, to help with those things that are. There is great comfort in this. Nothing will be beyond God and us to accomplish. Detachment from those situations and people we are not in charge of are examples of where He will come to our aid.

Taking a deep breath and allowing God to enter into our consciousness (He is always waiting, you know) is the first step to finding the courage and the willingness to detach, even when we want desperately to interfere. God will let us interfere, of course; we do have free will. But our desire for peace, if great enough, will help us make a wiser choice, one to which God says *amen*.

Bringing to mind whatever your vision of God is—whether it's a bright light, a hovering angel, a wise old man, a gentle breeze, or a field of wildflowers—will give you time to regroup when your ego is pushing you to control the uncontrollable. Relationships are never strengthened when we are playing God. Let's turn that job over to the One who has that title.

◆

God will always help us with any task that is ours.
Detachment is among those tasks that are.

## Detachment will require major changes for some, minor changes for others.

HAVE YOU NOTICED HOW SOME PEOPLE SEEM TO THOUGHT-lessly mind the business of others? We referred to them as the nosey neighbors when we were kids. They snooped, criticized, and gossiped. Perhaps you learned these traits as a youngster, too. When we carry them into adulthood, however, it doesn't bode well for our relationships. Observing the behaviors of others, whether we approve of them or not, is the only kind of atten-tion we should be giving. What they are doing is really none of our concern. This is not an easy lesson to learn. Begin by simply watching, saying nothing, and praying for the willingness to ac-cept them as they are.

Fortunately, we don't have to change this or any ill-conceived behavior instantaneously. We can inch toward the ultimate change we want to make, one day at a time. The accumulation of attempts will add up, and we will become the people we want to be, eventually.

No one wants to be thought of as pushy or controlling or nosey. There is only one way to forge the new us, and it's by liv-ing, one day at a time, with a new set of rules about how we will interact with everyone else. Nothing about our lives will feel the same once we begin to apply these suggestions.

✦

If life isn't peaceful 24/7, it could be because we are minding
the business of others, or trying to. Detaching from them in
all respects is the solution. This may be a big change for us
or a small one. But the size isn't relevant; the decision is.

Detaching from the chaos around us
by seeking the silence within creates
healing in us and in others too, in time.

163

CHAOS REIGNS EVERYWHERE. AT SOME TIME EVERY DAY, most of us will be bombarded by chaos we create or which is triggered by others close to us. The chaos in another part of the globe affects us, too. This may seem farfetched, but I don't doubt it anymore. Far too many spiritual practitioners are proponents for me to question the validity of this idea.

This transference of energy from one place to another is called the "butterfly effect." It means that what happens here will have its impact on the other side of the world, in due time, and vice versa. This isn't troubling, from my perspective; it's actually helpful because it means the good, along with the chaos, makes its mark. And when we are aware of the strength of the effect, we can put forth more of the good to soften the world at large.

We don't have to add to the strife anywhere, not at home, in our neighborhoods, or in our region of the world. Instead, we can add to the peace everywhere. It takes only a moment of silence and peaceful intention to begin the ripple of quiet hope that will be felt everywhere.

✦

Going into the silence is the most obvious way to detach
from people who are hounding us, or from situations that
are out of control. Silence is a solution. Always. A peaceful,
rewarding one.

The most effective way of keeping our focus where it belongs is by detaching from others.

WHERE DOES OUR FOCUS BELONG? THAT'S THE QUESTION we must address in hundreds of situations on a weekly basis. Our attention is easily snagged, following one scenario and then another, and we lose track of ourselves. Attending to the needs of others isn't necessarily wrong, but when it's at the expense of our own needs, we are creating more harm than good.

We must put ourselves first, and that doesn't mean we are being selfish. It means, simply, that we are honoring the journey we have been invited to travel, and we can't get to where we need to be if we get off the path too often to help those who need to be making their own way. That's the significant point: everyone must make his or her own way. We can love, support, even make suggestions, perhaps, but we can't take the reins from someone else. Hanging on to our own reins is the only assignment we must remain committed to.

There is only one way to accomplish what I am suggesting here: detach from the journey of others. That does not mean being unconcerned or unloving. On the contrary, detaching from others so that they can discover their own lessons and successes is one of the most loving acts we can perform.

◆

Staying focused on ourselves takes great effort when we first try it, but it does get easier, as does any new behavior. The payoff is well worth it. So every day, we must pull back if we find ourselves getting involved in situations that don't concern us.

If we fail to detach from a person who is always in turmoil, we're likely to blame them for our unhappiness.

ALLOWING THE IRRESPONSIBLE BEHAVIOR OR INSANE TUR-moil surrounding someone else to become the focus of how we are feeling in the moment is a prime setup for a resentment. We all know how this feels. Choosing to blame others for our lack of peace is commonplace. But we are in charge of our feelings! No one else's behavior has the power to determine our feelings, but we succumb, quite often, to this mindset. Many of us learned this from our parents, no doubt. And we can unlearn it.

The choice to detach is as available to us as is the choice to blame; we simply have practiced blaming more frequently. We can reset our default position, however, with a simple decision. It has occurred to me that learning how to detach is one of the reasons we are in pretty continual contact with others. Detachment is a "tool" that can be used not just with our families and friends but with strangers too.

Perhaps once a day we are faced with a situation with a stranger in which his behavior leaves us upset. It's in these instances that detachment comes in very handy. Nothing anyone else does ever has to send us reeling. Isn't that an empowering idea? It means that every day can be as joyful and as unencumbered as we choose to make it.

◆

Blaming others is a common habit. We see it played out in our families and between world powers, too. Allowing for our differences is one way to reduce our need to blame. Acceptance of the value that our differences bring to the table could change the tenor of every relationship, worldwide.

Every moment provides a chance for us
to make a healthy choice. Detachment
is one of the healthiest of all.

THIS MIGHT SEEM LIKE AN ODD SUGGESTION, BUT OUR attachment to others can prevent us from taking care of our personal needs: physical, emotional, mental, and spiritual. When that's the case, we may well succumb to ill health. Many members of the medical profession now agree that more than 90 percent of all sickness is related to stress. One of the biggest contributors to stress, I think, is our obsession with trying to control the actions and details of others' lives, those very details that we need to detach from and that are forever uncontrollable anyway.

It's an exciting realization that moment by moment we can change our perception, and a changed action will follow. We don't have to keep doing what we have always done. It's easy to stay in one groove, and we have made many of them very smooth by now, but it's exhilarating to know that we can cut a new swath. That's the opportunity we have every moment, in fact. We can head in a new direction, make a new decision, see our partners in a new way. Seeing our partners as our opportunities to learn new behaviors makes every experience with them very special.

After deciding to do anything in a new way, whether it's as mundane as taking a new route to work or joining an exercise program, just knowing that we have the power to make the change is its own pat on the back. Now let's not stop with the simple changes. Let's tackle the bigger ones, too.

◆

Let's take some time to watch others today. Do we see
enmeshment or detachment? The difference is pretty
obvious. Which do we want to emulate?

DETACHMENT IS NOT A SKILL WE ARE BORN WITH. IN FACT, we are born much more prone to clinging to others because of our uncertainties about life. As children, we often continue to cling, and our parents try to help us understand that we are safe, even when not in their presence. But for some of us, the insecurity lasts into adulthood and the clinging does, too. Fortunately, most of our companions resist our need to cling, and it becomes necessary for us to learn new behavior. Detachment is that new behavior.

The value of detachment is seldom obvious initially. One thing is certain: not letting the presence of others take charge of your life means they may not notice your presence at all, and that can be troubling. Maybe we don't want to be invisible. But it became obvious to me, many years ago, that my clinging, my trying to make myself indispensable to others, didn't prevent me from being invisible to them anyway. Their need of me precluded their desire to value my presence.

But what's to be done about this dilemma? We want to be valued. We want peaceful lives. We want to know we have made a difference in this world. But there are some activities that just won't guarantee it, and one of these is trying to be the absolute all to someone else. Prayer is a great way to break the temptation. It might actually be the only way to start the process. That's how it worked for me.

✦

Praying to be relieved of the need to cling is a worthy prayer. It might be a way to jump-start the habit of detachment.

Watching others will reveal to us
many who practice detachment.

WE HAVE ALL HEARD THE PHRASE "WHEN THE STUDENT IS ready, the teacher appears." This axiom also holds true for the practice of detachment. We are surrounded by people who seem generally unruffled by the behavior of others. The Dalai Lama and President Obama come to mind. Certain people seem able to let others do and say whatever they want to without having their own responses ruffled by them.

There are also those who are constantly in turmoil because someone isn't behaving the way they want them to. Count me as guilty of falling into this category. But I am moving up the learning curve. I am not where I was a few years ago, and by next year I won't be where I am now. Every time I see another person peacefully observing a situation without reacting, it gives me the momentum to continue my progress. And I know that my example is serving and inspiring others, too—those others who are lower on the curve than I am right now.

It's rather exciting to know that our teachers are everywhere. If we're not sure who they might be, we ask ourselves what it is we are trying to master. Then our teachers become apparent.

◆

It is such good news to know that there is no timeline in learning how to successfully detach. We have as much time as we need and as many teachers as we need. Our job is to watch for them.

Detaching from the struggles of
our loved ones does not preclude
witnessing their humanity.

169

BEING A WITNESS TO SOMEONE ELSE'S LIFE IS ONE OF THE
most loving gifts we can offer. Witnessing, however, does not
require us to get involved in the details of what anyone else is
doing. On the contrary, getting involved at that level is not ever
what we're expected to do, from a spiritual perspective. Observation is a way to acknowledge another's existence; it says, "I see
you," but nothing more.

Perhaps it doesn't seem like enough to simply witness the
life of a loved one. But the feeling of invisibility is haunting,
and many have dealt with that for decades. I, for one, felt very
alone and invisible, and thus turned to alcohol at age thirteen. It's
never our job to prevent others from taking that same route, but
perhaps it won't even appeal to them if they are on someone's
radar screen.

Keeping someone in our focus is not the same as *making*
them our focus. The former is kind and appropriate; the latter is
stunting and controlling. Let's make the right choice when we
witness another.

◆

We are living among our many loved ones by design. Having
the courage to witness their lives, rather than trying to
control them, is our assignment.

WHEN WE FREE OURSELVES FROM THE COMPULSION TO control others, we are indicating to them our acceptance of the choices they are making. It's not always easy to give up the compulsion, and it may not actually be "real," initially. "Acting as if" is an acceptable first step, however. Everyone needs to feel accepted as they are, and we can contribute to the level of personal satisfaction a person has if we simply "let them go" so that they can be themselves.

Everything we learn happens in stages. We don't become excellent at any skill after the first attempt. I well remember taking golf lessons a few years ago. I missed the ball more than I hit it. I still don't par very often, but I love the game and can see improvement. That's all we need to see, regardless of the skill we are practicing. Improvement keeps us coming back, they say. And coming back to the practice of detachment has innumerable rewards. Among them are peace, a sense of freedom, a quiet mind, and the awareness that others are more comfortable around us.

Letting others know we like them just as they are is a great compliment, one we all strive to experience. Let's remember that we must give away that which we want to receive, and acceptance will be our gift too.

◆

Taking today as the gift God is offering us to practice this most important of skills makes the desire to demonstrate detachment burn bright within. The first person who comes toward us is our next opportunity to practice. Use it.

# pause *and* reflect

Praying for willingness in every attempt to change our
    behavior is the first and most important step.
Blaming others for our unhappiness is so tempting.
We keep our focus where it belongs. There is little doubt
    about where that is.
When the chaos calls, leave.
Seeking the silence of our inner space is the solution when
    others are trying to entrap us in their madness.

We will always have at our fingertips God, the quiet within, and our journal if we need time away to sort out the confusion around us. Use one or all of these daily.

We are surrounded by other people who practice the art of detachment quite well. They are present to show us it can be done. Watch them carefully. What do we see? Make a plan to mimic their behavior. Ask them for help. That's why they are there!

We let our hope grow that we can become examples for others, too. That's one of the greatest aspects of our journey.

WHEN WE MAKE THE DECISION TO DETACH FROM THE antics of others, whether those others are complete strangers or, more commonly, our loved ones, we are saving ourselves from the emotional turmoil that can follow our ill-conceived reactions. Taking that crucial moment to step away from the situation in order to consider a healthy response (perhaps no response at all) shows the kind of growth we all long for. Making this choice isn't really as hard as it first may seem.

Reacting to the craziness of so many people who share our path may be second nature. We watched it in our family of origin. We see it in the film industry and on myriad television shows. We see it played out on the local and national stage, too. Staying comfortably in one's own skin, undisturbed by anyone else's actions, is an art form.

Occasionally we observe this healthy behavior in a friend. When we consider those leaders we most admire, we see it too—in Mandela and Martin Luther King, for example. They each had a mission and were driven to move toward it, undeterred by all those individuals who tried to draw them into conflict. Their examples prove that we all can do as they did. It's about perseverance, willingness, and practice. Practicing a new behavior can be an exciting challenge if we approach it from that perspective.

◆

Challenge is good; we are all improved by it. Deciding exactly how we will act in every circumstance we are faced with today, rather than falling back to a timeworn reaction, is a challenge that we can handle. The world will be better for it.

Are you choosing to detach when the
opportunity presents itself today?

172

EVERY MINUTE OF EVERY DAY, UNLESS WE ARE LIVING IN complete isolation, offers us an opportunity to get involved in a situation or to stand back from it. Some situations should involve us, particularly if decisions that affect us are being made. But much that is going on around us doesn't need our input. We are bystanders who can choose to simply observe what others are saying and doing. For many of us, this seems next to impossible. We clearly think that our suggestions are key to others making the best decisions. How wrong that thought is.

It's such a good practice to allow others to be in charge of their own lives, which includes their own decisions. Perhaps our own parents or friends got too invested in our lives, developing in us the idea that interference wasn't necessarily bad and surely not unexpected. It may even be helpful on occasion. No one of us can see the big picture all the time. But making the choice to be a bystander, unless our expertise is specifically sought, is a safer, saner decision. Our own lives give us plenty to be concerned with.

◆

Being selective about where we place out attention and what we say will make us grateful at day's end. We don't have to do what we always did. Today is a new day.

## 173 There is a subtle distinction between joining with those on our journey and detaching from them when we need to.

OUR DESIRE TO HEAL SPIRITUALLY, EMOTIONALLY, AND oftentimes physically is enhanced when we recognize our similarities with others rather than our differences. The decision to join means to put aside our comparisons and criticisms and seek, instead, to see how we can complement one another on this path we are sharing. That is what God, however we define Him, hopes for us as well. We can be the way-showers as well as the students, and all of us move forward as a result.

The importance of coming together with others should not be misinterpreted, however. Joining forces to help one another heal is not the same as trying to control one another's healing. We are not in charge of anything as it relates to someone else. Our own lives are all that deserve our undivided attention.

What does this mean, practically? It means we allow ourselves to be empathetic, to be kind and accepting and available if our loved one wants to seek strength, experience, and hope from us. But it does not mean we are in the driver's seat of anyone else's bus. We witness and then share our thoughts if they are sought. A prayer or two is always appropriate, however. All of us benefit from every prayer.

✦

Living in concert with others is one of the great pleasures of being alive. It can also be one of the setups for frustration. Knowing when to join forces and when we should let others alone is what we are here to learn. The opportunities will be prevalent today.

There is one sure way to experience peace: detach from the upheavals of others.

174

UNLESS WE ARE LIVING IN AN ASHRAM, WE WILL NOT likely be able to avoid conflict. It happens. We have all seen the research that establishes that when any two people observe the same accident, they seldom agree on exactly what happened. Our personal lives influence how we see and then how we interpret what we observe, or even read. In many instances this is good. It can make for richness in our relationships and discussions with friends as well as our adversaries. But it can also lead to conflict.

Conflict isn't a problem for some. I know individuals who seem to thrive on it. I knew a man a few years ago who began every day by reading the headlines or watching the news, getting agitated over the state of the union, and then going from house to house trying to incite an argument. It was strange, but he seemed to need this in order to feel alive. He certainly was not in search of peace. Unfortunately, he died of a heart attack at a relatively early age. I am not sure this habit had contributed to it, but it couldn't have helped his health.

The desire for peace is far more appealing to me than having an intense discussion, even when the conversation isn't a full-blown argument. I steer clear of conflict whenever I can. The practice of detachment has helped me to do this. Growing up in a conflict-ridden family no doubt influences how I still respond to tense situations sometimes. But peaceful emotions are much more satisfying to me. The upside of this is that I am far more willing to detach from some situations, and that pleases me.

◆

Being at peace has grown even more important to me with age. I love a good discussion but not an argument. If peace appeals to you too, the practice of detaching from the viewpoints of others, when they conflict with yours, is the pathway to seek.

## The act of detachment precludes criticism.

CRITICISM ISN'T A STRANGER TO MOST OF US. YOU MIGHT
say it's a national pastime. Critics fill the opinion pages of most
newspapers. We hear it in our homes. Talk radio thrives on
criticism. We are seduced into criticizing our contemporaries
without even recognizing it. Unfortunately, it seems as natural
as breathing.

Are we so uncomfortable with the successes of others or
opinions that differ from ours that we have to judge people as
lesser in some way? I think most psychologists would say yes.
When others outshine us in some way, or we fear they are going
to do so, our own egos want to pull them back to make them
smaller than ourselves. What a struggle we have on our hands
when the ego does our thinking for us. It does not want us to
be equally in concert with others. Therefore, it has only one
reaction to make: criticize everyone.

Criticism doesn't have to be our only response to the people
around us, however. We can choose to believe that their successes benefit all of us. We can choose to believe that what
anyone else receives is a gift to all. We can remember that there
is always enough of everything to go around, so we don't have to
be jealous or feel inferior. All these feelings are available choices
to us. When we apply the power of detachment, we can access
whatever feeling we want because we are free from the emotional energy of the ego.

♦

When we free ourselves from the machinations of others, we
find we aren't inclined to criticize. When that's our choice,
we are adding to our inner peace as well as to the peace felt
throughout our communities. What a blessing we can be by
making this one tiny decision.

LIVING IN A STATE OF FEAR ABOUT WHAT OTHERS MIGHT choose to do next is an extremely uncomfortable way to live. Yet it's familiar. Some crave being the center of every circle; in this way, all relationships seem to feel secure to them. These fear-based people can't yet face how unrealistic this illusion of security actually is. They only know how to hang on and then pray that their partners don't break free.

Feeling as though a relationship is required is never a peaceful place to be. Wanting one is a reasonable enough desire, but needing one keeps you from breathing deeply and peacefully during the individual moments as they pass by. And life is made up of individual moments, nothing more, in fact.

When fear is the primary feeling you have, no individual moment will allow your heart to be peaceful. No individual moment will allow you to lovingly notice the others on your path as free people, not hostages. And if we can't see them as free, we can't see them at all.

◆

Being attached to others isn't really living. When we hang on too tightly, our journey is hindered and our hopes will never be fulfilled. That's not an easy concept, perhaps, but we need to grasp it in order to grow.

**Do we want freedom to grow or a life that's small? How we relate to others determines this.**

MOST PEOPLE WOULD SAY THEY NOT ONLY WANT TO GROW but that they expect to grow within their relationships. They see interactions with their companions throughout the day as the avenues for that growth. But what I frequently observe is many people living the way I lived for so long: hanging on to every one of the people in my life, certain that if I let them have their own lives, separate from me, that I would be discarded. My pain of those years has not been forgotten. I can see that same pain on the faces of many I walk among.

I don't want to suggest that I have graduated to a higher level of being, but I have learned some very important lessons over the years that have changed everything about the way I feel within my relationships. I have learned that the companions I have chosen have also chosen me. I have learned that what I need to know is being offered every day, sometimes through a challenge, other times through an answer to a prayer. I have learned that when I let go of those companions and let them live their lives, trusting that they will still be the teachers I need, I will experience the peace that I deserve.

It's within the peaceful heart that continued growth happens most easily. We can force ourselves to grow in certain ways, perhaps, but it's hard to sustain any growth if we have had to force it. Detaching from what is affecting someone else is the avenue to the peace we need in order to demonstrate to them that peace is possible.

◆

Today is a new beginning, every day is. Do we want a day of growth that we can look to with pride? If so, we must keep our sights on ourselves, not on the lives of others.

Making the decision to change
how we think can open the door
to the practice of detachment.

178

WHEN OUR EXPERIENCES WITH OTHERS ARE PAINFUL, many of us try to tolerate those persons rather than try to change those aspects of ourselves that could be changed. The anticipation of the unknown, that is, a change we might make, can seem more fraught with pain than what we have learned to accept within our current situations. Does this sound familiar? I certainly lived in this space of painful acceptance for decades.

Until I wandered into Twelve Step recovery rooms, I had no idea that there was another way to live. I actually thought that my choices were limited and had already been made, for all time. I am embarrassed to admit this, but I was convinced that if others changed, I could have a good life. Being told that I could never count on someone else to change depressed me, terribly. And then I heard how joyous others were with the changes that they had opted to make for themselves.

We do learn from the others on our path that our possibilities are unlimited. I was like a sponge, a great imitator of those people I watched who had peaceful lives, for the most part. What they did, which I had never tried, was to keep the focus on themselves. They made plans for who and what they wanted their lives to be. They did not create lives around the plans of others. It had simply never occurred to me that I could have my very own life and that it would not preclude my loving others, too. Since learning this, nothing about my life has stayed the same.

✦

We are never too old to learn how to live more peacefully.
Letting others live however they choose is a first step.

## Appreciating the gift and the power of detachment is certain to lead us to a simpler life.

As I've said already, I had never heard about de-TACHment until I came into recovery rooms. I was a very slow learner. I was afraid to let go of the people I considered significant to my life. Abandonment had been my biggest fear since childhood. What initially triggered that I'll never know, but it hung over me like a heavy, black drape.

When I saw the slogan "Let Go and Let God" hanging on the wall of the Alano Club, I was both agitated and confused. I wasn't sure I believed in God; and just how did one let go? What that meant was beyond my comprehension. Then I heard someone say, "I feel free, at last, since letting go of my son's decisions." I could see the peace registered on this person's face and hear it in her voice. That was a turning point for me.

I asked this woman to tell me, more specifically, what she had done and if she could coach me to do the same. My healing began that day, as did my application of the tool of detachment. I took only tiny steps at first, but every day I practiced.

Detachment is powerful, and it is a gift available to anyone who wants it. It's not an unloving act; it's a way of expressing greater love for yourself and other people. Since being introduced to detachment, my life has never looked or felt the same.

◆

If you want what some of us now claim for our daily lives, begin this practice today. It's life changing.

Detaching from the chaos of others' lives may not look like love, but it is.

180

LOVE SURELY WEARS MANY FACES. IT MIGHT BE EXPRESSED as an unexpected bouquet of yellow roses from a friend, or a handwritten note in these days of the Internet. Perhaps a call from a loved one who has been silent for a time lets you know they still care. Or maybe the love you'll experience today is as simple as a kind smile from a stranger at the grocery store. All these are memorable expressions.

But there's an entirely different expression of love too, one that I never would have considered in my youth: it's detachment, and it appears in many forms. For instance, ignoring the antics, the crazy chaos, that some of our loved ones create is one example of "loving" detachment. Another way to express it is by not doing for others the work that they need to be doing for themselves. Not getting people out of jams that they have created, even when it's hard to let them experience their own consequences, is love at its best, sometimes.

We may find it hard to understand that letting others "sink or swim" as they choose is love. But it is. The difficulty is that sometimes others don't end up "swimming," and then we have to remember that everyone has their own journey and their own Higher Power. Our assignment is to witness, to pray, and to hope, but never to do for someone else what they need to do.

✦

Detachment isn't for sissies, some would say, but it is for those who want to express love more fully in this short life that we share with our traveling companions.

# pause *and* reflect

Every day is rife with choices. Let's be careful regarding those
that we make.

We are the thinkers, the creators, of our thoughts. Thoughts
don't mysteriously appear in our minds. We change them
if we are not feeling peaceful.

The chaos that others choose to experience doesn't have to
garner our attention.

Unconditional love has many expressions. Detachment is
one of them.

We cling to people when we are afraid. Seek God, instead, in
those moments.

What's the most valuable tool you use within your
relationships currently? Is it offering you the peace you
deserve? If you are agitated, ever, you are trying to control,
and peace never visits the controller. Take a few moments,
now, to reenvision yourself in your most significant relationships. Who do you want to be? How do you see yourself in your best moments? Now meditate on this picture
every day for a week and watch the changes transpire.

Detaching from our friends spurs some
of them on to being more responsible.

181

RESPONSIBILITY FOR OUR LIVES IS ONE OF THE KEY LES-
sons we are here to learn. Many of us grew up in families that
didn't encourage much independence, so our learning curve has
been steep. If we team up with friends and lovers who caretake
too much, we still fail to master the tools that allow us to live
self-directed, responsible lives.

It's not up to us to make anyone else responsible, but we can
coax a friend's journey along the right path by being certain that
we are not doing for them what they need to do for themselves.
Recognizing the boundaries between us is a first, necessary step.
Respecting those boundaries does not mean creating a false separation between us, but understanding that we do have unique
qualities and unique lessons and celebrating that fact.

The principle of detachment is a great tool both for the one
working it and for the one on the receiving end. When we detach from someone else, we lift our own spirit considerably. This
may not seem to be the case at first, but as we grow more accustomed to the freedom we feel, we will know that what we have
done for the other person, as well as for ourselves, was the right
thing. And we will want to repeat the exercise again and again.

◆

That's the hope of this exercise—that it will be repeated
and imitated and cherished. Our homes, our communities,
and even the discussions that are held among world leaders
would be far different if this exercise were practiced. A very
small change in one's demeanor can have a very big impact
over time.

**A sure indication that we have not embraced detachment is when our focus is too much on someone else.**

I MENTIONED IN AN EARLIER MEDITATION THAT I USED to spend hours every day obsessing over what others might be thinking of me. I even watched the faces of total strangers to see if they were noticing me and, if they were, wondering if they were thinking positive thoughts. Of course, my focus on my significant partner (of the moment) was sizzling with intensity.

Perhaps I was simply sicker than most young women. I do know that I carried this doubt from my childhood into my adulthood, and were it not for what I have learned from other wiser people, I'd still be trapped in that most fearful existence. It doesn't matter if my struggle was rooted in my family of origin. Learning how to detach was one of the lessons I came here to learn, regardless, and having my family play its role in this was appropriate.

Attachment to others and what they might be thinking, coupled with analyzing how our behavior might change that thinking, is a great definition for codependence. Many suffer from it. But there is a solution, and if we opt to follow it, we will get a daily reprieve from our obsession with any other person. The solution is this: acknowledge that your appropriate role in someone else's life is kindness and prayer, perhaps sharing an experience when asked, and then wishing them well with no strings attached. Then turn to the only life you can control: your own.

◆

Flip-flopping between our own life and someone else's means no life gets the attention it deserves. Since we can only take good care of one life, let's choose wisely today.

THE DICTIONARY DEFINES *DETACHMENT* AS "DISPASSION"
or "disinterest." In some cases that might be an appropriate
definition, but in this book *detachment* means letting go, allowing
the object of one's attention to make his or her own decisions or
mistakes. We can and, in most cases, will still be very interested
in the person and his choices, but reacting to them is what we're
trying to refrain from doing. Not reacting does not mean not
caring. For many of us this is a new awareness.

What might we do today if we had only ourselves to think
about? In reality, we can have that kind of day every day. That
doesn't mean we have quit caring about the well-being of others. It means that we are keeping our attention where it needs
to be, while letting others be in charge of themselves. We walk
*beside* our companions, not in front of or behind or within the
same footprints. We join one another on the trek through life,
but we don't chart each other's course. That's a significant point,
not to be overlooked.

I have observed some people who use detachment as a way
of reprimanding others, more or less. That behavior continues
to hold both people hostage. The kind of detachment I am pro-
posing here is soft and gentle and honorable. It says, "I trust you
to make your decisions. And I will comment if you so choose."

✦

Letting someone know we do believe in their capacity
to live fully without our interference is a gift as great as a
college degree, to some. Let's make sure we are fulfilling the
role we are here to play.

It's not easy for a person who constantly seeks the attention of others to be "ignored." Some think they need to be the center of everyone's world. And when they are surrounded by people who get their good feelings from taking care of others, a very unhealthy dynamic is created. Perhaps some of us reading this have participated on one side of this drama or the other. As I recall my past, I played both parts, often, and to no one's benefit.

I thought that if I took good care of someone I'd never be rejected. I both wanted to be the center of that peron's life and wanted him to be the center of mine. When relationship after relationship ended, I was devastated. What was it that I was failing to do? Fortunately, I finally got introduced to detachment as a loving expression. And my life has been better ever since.

What did detachment do for me? It gave me a life of my own. It allowed me to let others live unencumbered by my attention. I began to grow and have confidence in my separate abilities, and I discovered that there was a plan for me that didn't include taking care of others in the way I always had. Having my own plan didn't mean others were no longer important. It meant that their presence in my life was a complement to my journey, not the center of it. Only in this way do all parties get to live the life they have been born to experience.

◆

Love wears many cloaks. Detachment is just one of them.
When we wrap ourselves in detachment, it will soften the day.

Surrendering your control over life,
your own life and the lives of others, is a
great demonstration of detachment.

It takes an act of courage to surrender the out-come of the affairs of one's life. Being told that the effort is mine but not the outcome was not an idea I easily grasped when I first heard it. I had been used to thinking that my skill as a manager of a company made me a natural at controlling outcomes.

What I learned, and I think what we all have to learn, is that the management of certain tasks still doesn't guarantee that the outcome we are shooting for will be successful. And the quicker we come to appreciate the role that surrender can play in our lives, the more peaceful every moment will be.

Surrendering control doesn't mean not caring how a situation might turn out. It means trusting that whatever happens is "acceptable" and can be appreciated, if not now, then in due time. We call this kind of surrender detachment. It's not a negative reaction; it's quite the opposite, in fact. Surrendering to the forces outside ourselves allows us to enjoy, with much greater satisfaction, every single moment of every day.

✦

Equating detachment with surrendering offers a clarification
we may have missed. Letting either term guide us will free
us, which creates the peace we all deserve.

Our willingness to detach from others
is enhanced if we have developed
trust in a Higher Power.

TRUSTING A HIGHER POWER IS EASIER FOR SOME THAN FOR
others. Having a specific experience that convinces us that God
was actually present makes a difference. I had more than one of
those experiences in early recovery from my addictions, which
was fortunate because I had not grown up as a believer. But
the message I received was too powerful to ignore. My Higher
Power actually provided the words for me to say (as though the
words were being said for me, in fact) in a situation that was far
too daunting for me to have handled alone. My seed of trust was
planted then. It has been sustained ever since.

The power of that experience convinced me that everyone
has a connection to their own God, and I am not that God for
anyone. Trusting that this is true makes it far easier for me to
walk away from the situations that have captured the attention
of another person. As I have already said, walking away doesn't
mean we don't care. We simply don't have to get involved in
how others resolve their situations. They need to rely on their
God for guidance and get the empowerment from the process
that I and many other people have gotten.

Detachment may look like disinterest to some because of the
act of walking away or looking beyond a situation in which a
friend is trapped. But it's closely allied with trust. Trusting that
God will do for others what God always does for us when we
wait patiently. Having hope for our friend is the best we can
offer him.

✦

Consider any time, large or small, when God "showed up"
for you. Let that memory guide you to allow the same to
be true for all your companions today. You need not do for
them what they should be doing with God's help.

Detachment can feel like lack of love.
But it's really God's will.

187

EQUATING DETACHMENT WITH GOD'S WILL MAY SEEM sacrilegious, but it's a unique and very cogent way of understanding the concept once we get beyond the religious overtones we might attach to God's will. Perhaps the notion of God's will is more accessible if we think of it as an expression of love. God does will for us to love one another. And ourselves. One of the best expressions of our love for one another is to show support and concern but remain distant from the problems someone else needs to resolve. That distance is called detachment.

Remaining detached actually allows for greater love, I think, because our own emotions don't begin to dictate what the other person should be doing, thus clouding the impact of our silent though very powerful expression. Sitting in quiet prayer on behalf of someone else when they are struggling may seem like a cold act, but it is fulfilling God's will for our lives in that moment. Every person needs to establish his or her own relationship with God. It's not our job to introduce them

We have fewer tasks to complete in this life than we might have surmised, but that's because so many of us thought we had to do our work and someone else's work, too. But we are just as busy; the nature of the work has simply changed. Prayer comes first, then mediation, and if there are any specific assignments, they will be shown to us. We can be certain that they will not include doing the work someone else needs to do.

✦

Our love for our fellow humans is expressed most gloriously
when we move our words aside and simply witness,
listen, and pray.

# 188

Dreams can help us in our development
of any skill. Detachment is one of them.

THERE ARE SLEEPING DREAMS AND WAKING DREAMS. I AM
referring here to dreams we have while awake, which might
be even more significant to most of us since we can remember
them in detail and experience them quite intentionally. I think
that when we want to hone any skill, imagining ourselves as
being skillful in that area, in quiet contemplation, quite surpris-
ingly helps us improve the level of skill we have. Psychologists
agree, as I stated earlier.

Applying this idea to the development of detachment may
seem unusual to some of us. But individuals whose emotions
easily get entangled in the lives of others will come to appreciate
being accomplished at this skill. It makes so much difference in
how we feel on a daily basis. And it allows for greater personal
achievement when we aren't caught up in someone else's lack
of achievement.

Our attention to others isn't always with those we love or
even know, but our emotions can get triggered anyway. Perhaps
we observed an irate customer in a grocery store and we felt
anger slowly rising in us. Figuring out how to detach from this
scenario is good practice. Those situations we can't control—
and that includes most of life—have to be turned away from. In
time we will be able to do this peacefully.

✦

The development of detachment as a skill will pay off
however we accomplish it. Don't give up trying until the
miracle occurs.

Making the commitment to detach
from our loved ones (and all others
too) is a big change for many of us.

189

OUR PARENTS MAY HAVE BEEN OVERLY INVOLVED IN OUR lives as children. If so, this may have set an unfortunate example of what is appropriate behavior. It's not unusual for parents to care, and they should, but allowing children to experience their own lives, make their own mistakes, and decide their own goals without the constant supervision of parents or other adults is good. If our parents' wishes overly shadowed our lives, we will struggle to let our offspring, our friends, or our lovers have the independence they need.

Love does not mean being dependent on others or having others dependent on us. Love is best understood as interdependence: coming together when that's what will make us strong and remaining apart when individual goals need attention. If we feel being attached to others enhances our comfort level, we may need to step back and consider the strain that attachment is actually putting on the dreams of both parties.

Detaching from the challenges or the successes of others allows them to discover how to handle the host of experiences that are being presented to them. We each have our own, and we each must do our own. There really is no mystery to this idea. Let go of others. That's all detachment means. And it's possible.

✦

When I first heard about detaching, I thought, "no way." I was certain I'd never be able to allow for someone's independence. My own success has been greatly enhanced since first giving it a try. What has happened for me can happen for anyone. Take a chance. Today.

## 190 Being willing to practice the art of detachment is what promises us the freedom to grow.

WE CANNOT BE FULLY FOCUSED ON TWO PEOPLE AT THE same time. And many of us don't respect that we need to be our number one priority. This is a delicate situation, however. So let me be clear: this is not an invitation to discount others or to ignore them when the gentle act of listening could offer them some healing support and possibly teach us something very important at the same time. We have already established that our encounters are never accidental. We must notice them! But the intention is for an exchange, a teaching opportunity that benefits both people, and then the ripple effect will carry the lesson to others, too.

Having a learning experience with others—and all encounters are learning experiences—doesn't preclude our staying focused primarily on the growth that is assuredly tucked in the experience for us. We can't know what another person's lesson is. We can only assume that there is one, because we have been brought together. There are no accidents. Our growth has been charted for us ahead of time. We simply must be willing to make room for it, and a life that is too focused on someone else's lessons fails to accomplish its own.

◆

Detachment equals freedom and growth and peace of mind. Could we want any more than that?

# pause *and* reflect

Where has our focus been lately? If it's been on someone else, it's time to refocus.

Our own life goes wanting if we mind someone else's business.

Sit quietly in the company of others as practice. We don't have to speak. How freeing this realization is.

Giving our loved ones over to God is a great gift to them. And an even better gift to us.

How would you rank your level of peace right now? Is it where you want it to be? If not, reread some of the preceding lessons and make a plan for what you can do right now to give yourself greater peace. Don't let another day go by when you are caught in the throes of chaos or dissatisfaction with yourself or others. We don't ever have to live in that space! The choice to live in total peace is ours.

THERE ARE SO MANY TIMES IN OUR LIVES THAT SILENCE
is just waiting to be embraced. Some consider walking through
the woods a time of silence. When silent, we can hear the birds
calling to one another, perhaps warning a mother bird that
danger is present. Sitting by a lake, hearing only the occasional
canoe slip by or the duck that is quacking to gather her babies
to the shore, is another such time. The gifts we experience from
times like these, if savored, live long in our hearts.

The ability we have to return to these memories when the
turmoil of a situation is getting under our skin can shift our
perception instantly. And shifting our perception is the ultimate
gift, I think. Some call it a miracle. We don't ever have to stay in
the turmoil, either someone else's or our own. We can see it but
stand outside of it. We can seek to see it differently, too. Or we
can walk away, knowing that it's a reflection of a mindset and has
only the reality and importance that we give it.

Detaching from the turmoil that has been created by anyone
becomes easier every time we remember to do it. And the empowerment we feel each time we detach makes choosing this
option more attractive the next time.

◆

Savoring a few moments of silence on a daily basis can
make a big difference in how the day unfolds. And seeking
it, too, when tension is triggered, doubles the freedom
we can feel. Don't let another day go by without a few
quiet moments.

Sharing a path in life doesn't mean
stepping on each other's toes.

192

HAVE YOU EVER WISHED YOUR SPOUSE COULD READ YOUR mind? I have. But if we take this to the next level, do we really want them to know what we are thinking all the time? I doubt it. Rather, we want our way, and we don't want to have to plead or manipulate or bargain for it. We want it freely given to us. But life is about compromise and negotiation and letting go. That's how we all grow and learn from one another. Simply having others give in isn't good for either party. Resentments can build, which usually spells trouble in the relationship.

That we have companions is wonderful, and that they have been selected to join us is an idea worth cherishing. We are meant to share this journey with them, for now, at least. There must be a lesson involved. The question is, are we ready to absorb it? Are we willing to accept what it's telling us? For many, the primary lesson is learning that we each have a plan to fulfill and must step back to allow it to unfold. Stepping in front of or on someone else's plan will never be part of our plan. Never.

Some say that our journeys with our specific companions never end, that we will meet again in another setting. We can't know that when living in this moment, but it's an intriguing idea, one that pleases me. I like to think that if I stepped on someone's toes in the past, I can right that wrong sometime in our future.

✦

I have had some tough relationships. Trusting that I selected them to get what I needed to learn pleases me and lessens the blows of them. How about you?

**193**   Our greatest asset in life is having God's
presence, whether it's to help us detach
from others or simply to breathe.

As a child I never seriously considered whether God was "real." I think God and Santa Claus fell into the same category in my mind: they were worth dreaming about occasionally but could not be relied upon. I gave up believing in Santa in the second grade. I never really sought the help of God at all until my thirties. And then it was out of desperation, not with any initial commitment to developing a relationship.

Now I am grateful for the desperate straits I was in because of the value of what I have learned. My loss of a husband, coupled with my addictions, turned my life into chaos. God, along with the Twelve Steps, were presented as possible solutions. I have never looked back.

Out of the ashes of tragedy, new life is always born, I think. My introduction to powerlessness was my first segue into the concept of detachment, and that has been a guiding force and strength in my life ever since. Maybe I'd have eventually been introduced to detachment and the freedom it promises through another set of circumstances. I'll never know. But having begun to gather the fruits of its application a few years ago, I know my life has been enriched almost beyond my wildest dreams.

I share my joy with you so that you can begin to claim these fruits, too. We all deserve lives of peace and joy and freedom. There is nothing stopping this from happening but ourselves.

✦

There is no better time than this moment to claim the help
that's waiting for us because of the presence of God within.
We wait no longer.

The recognition of another person's need
for space helps us develop our own commitment to the healing value of detachment.

194

PERHAPS WE HAVE TO VALUE OUR OWN PERSONAL SPACE before we can truly value another's right to have it, too. Or maybe the two happen simultaneously. But understanding that each one of us deserves privacy, the right to make decisions unencumbered, the freedom to say "Thanks, but no thanks" to any offering of help is a major step in truly understanding why we have crossed paths in the first place. We are here to teach one another. This has always been true, and it always will be. The teachers change, but the fact remains.

We have to be in the vicinity of one another, I think, to be able to see that we also need to turn away on occasion. That may seem odd when we first consider it, but unless others are around, we don't appreciate the importance of being apart from them, too. We must assert ourselves, if necessary, and we must allow our companions to do likewise, without taking it personally. Detach= ment is not a personal attack. It's the key to helping someone else, and ourselves too, to develop more fully.

Although some may interpret what appears to be disinterest as a personal affront, in time it will be understood for what it is: the door that's swinging open to a healthy you.

◆

Appreciating those times when others leave us alone is a sign that we are advancing up the learning curve. Having others detach from us is as important as our detaching from them.

## 195 Sometimes we resist detaching from the problems of others because reacting feels so good.

THE ATTRACTION TO YELLING AT SOMEONE FOR THEIR failure to handle a problem is overwhelming sometimes. And if we have a slip and yell, even though we can't take back our words, we can make amends and remove ourselves from the situation, rather than make it worse. The simple fact is that we were probably raised by parents who reacted to everything we did, and in our school systems, that's how order was maintained. Having been the product of so much reaction in our lives, we were imprinted, you might say, with the notion that reacting is the right way to express ourselves.

Reaction, which is often violent and thoughtless, is meted out by cops and gang members on a regular basis. Very seldom does someone in the seat of authority take time to consider an appropriate *action;* rather, a swift *reaction* is the norm. Even though generally we are not the authority over others, we may still fall back on the kind of response we experienced so often in our impressionable years.

But we can make another choice. Unfortunately, it will feel unfamiliar initially. So why should we make it? Because it will feel far better, eventually. We will experience a quiet peacefulness, in time, and we will see that our changed behavior fosters a change in others too, in time.

◆

There is no time like right now to say, "Enough with the old, in with the new," and begin to think through what we want to say and do before doing it. And when we aren't sure, we do nothing!

If we want freedom from our addiction to
controlling others, prayer is the solution,
and detachment is the result.

IF WE PUSH OTHERS TO BE WHO WE WANT THEM TO BE,
if we are invested in their successes, if we feel that their failures
are a reflection on us, then we are holding a book that can offer
some helpful guidance. I share in these meditations only what
has worked for me, drawn from my own experience, strength,
and hope. I have been a controller for much of my life. But my
trajectory is changing as the result of prayer and the trust it has
given me regarding the value of letting others go. I assure you
that your trajectory can change, too.

Freeing ourselves from our compulsion to control people,
places, and situations also frees everyone around us, and when
they feel that sense of freedom, they can, at last, become responsible, accountable individuals. Unfortunately, this doesn't happen
overnight. I have repeatedly had to recommit to prayer and the
willingness to give up control. Progress is evident, however, with
my companions who are experiencing greater freedom, and in
my prayer life.

Having a stronger prayer life has offered me payoffs in other
areas as well. I am more at peace. I feel more God-directed in
all ways, and my level of trust about the unfolding of my life has
made me a better listener, a more sincere witness to the lives of
others, and more confident. No gift has come my way that can't
also be yours.

✦

Prayer is the answer. We have heard this for years. The
resistance to believing it can hinder our journeys. Are you
ready to set aside your disbelief?

EVERY AL-ANON MEETING I HAVE EVER ATTENDED HAS had a host of wonderful teachers of detachment—men and women who have learned, oftentimes after years of pain and struggle, that their loved ones had to be allowed to make their own mistakes, their own choices, good or bad, sometimes choices that ultimately led to death, in fact. In the early years, I marveled at their courage and wondered if I'd ever get there. What the past few decades have shown me is that not only can we get there, but also our presence is what continues to show others that they can get there, too.

As I've said before, I believe that our primary role in each other's life is teaching. Whether it's to teach about detachment or acceptance or the many ways to express love, we are quite intentionally present to one another. This idea gives me a great sense of relief. There have been individuals on my path who I didn't necessarily like, but from them I often have learned great lessons, ones that served me well when I most needed a fresh perspective. Some refer to this shift in perspective as a miracle, and I like that notion. It means miracles aren't available to only a few, very special people. We can all claim them and discover a new source of strength that's never more than a new thought away.

◆

Knowing that our teachers are everywhere invites us to look at everyone who crosses our path with greater intention. The lessons aren't always obvious, but they are there. It took a while for detachment to get my attention, but the result of practicing it has been miraculous. The same will be true for you.

There is no time but now. Do we want
to peacefully enjoy it? Being willing
to detach from chaos is the way.

WHERE IS THE CHAOS IN YOUR LIFE? PERHAPS YOU THINK
there is none, but where was your mind just a moment before
opening this book? Was it quiet, or were you worrying about a
future event, a college examination, a doctor's appointment, or
a discussion with your boss? Maybe you are still hanging on to
a situation with a friend that upset you yesterday. Or maybe you
are living in fear of a conversation you know you need to have
with your spouse or one of your children. Not many of us live
in the quiet spaces very often. Let's not shame ourselves for that.
Instead, let's be willing to begin living another way.

And what is that other way? It's actually not very mysterious. In fact, as children we had it mastered. It's the art of paying
attention to what's in front of you and nothing else. Watch a
child in a sandbox. Nothing else matters to them, not even the
voice of their mother. It's not that the child doesn't care about
Mom; they are absorbed in play, in the trucks and the hill they
are scooping up for the truck to go over. Their attention is fully
engaged, and they have not a worry.

We can become like little children again. We can set aside all
else but the moment in front of us. It takes willingness to slow
down our thoughts and then quiet them completely. But mystics
have done it for eons. We can do it, too. And when we detach
from the extraneous messages running through our minds, we
will feel a slowed breath, a physical lightness, and a peace that
truly passes our former understanding.

✦

Remember, *Be Here Now*, a great book written by Ram Dass
more than three decades ago, was my first real introduction
to how one attains a quiet mind. With perseverance, it's not
hard. Be willing and watch life change around you. It will.

Detachment may seem antithetical to the
spiritual principle of joining. It's not.

WHEN WE DECIDE TO LET OTHERS MAKE THEIR OWN
choices, we may feel as though we have abandoned them. After
all, in many instances we have been trying to spin someone else's
cocoon their entire life. Letting them spin without us deprives
us of feeling needed, and that's what we crave. Our craving, if
left unchecked, prevents someone else from becoming the butterfly they are scheduled to be. And interestingly, we will never
become who we are meant to be, either, when our focus is so
entirely on them.

It's a vicious cycle. But we must let go so that we can come
together as we should. Joining, in the right way, is the real reason
for our being in each other's life, and that right way means being
on equal footing, as teachers and students simultaneously.

Being told that we have to detach, to let go, so that we can
join, does seem like a conundrum when we first hear it. But
with patience, we do come to understand that our unhealthy
attachment to someone, an attachment that strangles both of us,
has to be relinquished. And if we keep our hearts open, we do
come to understand the principle of joining, of coming together
as loving way-showers.

◆

Joining with our fellow travelers feels quietly good and
peacefully right. Trying to control someone feels restrictive
and unsatisfying because of their unyielding stance. Which is
the more sensible choice to make? I think it's obvious.

WE ARE BEING MOTIVATED BY FEAR OR LOVE IN EVERY encounter we experience. This may seem like an oversimplification, but I have found that it's the best way for me to judge my actions or reactions to others on my path. If I am able to observe people living however they choose, without it unduly upsetting me, then I am practicing acceptance, which is an act of love. If I am agitated by their actions, I am experiencing fear, and I want them to change.

Alas, we can't make anyone change. As we come to terms with this, we will be better able to accept people as they are, which is the first and necessary step that allows us to love them. Learning in programs like Al-Anon that our fear is what keeps us attached to someone, and that our own growth is narrowly restricted by our attachment, makes detachment a much more appealing consideration. But doing it is quite another thing. Taking it in small strides is a beginning.

Just for one day, acknowledge when you are feeling an inner dis-ease because of someone else's behavior and seek the willingness to back off. Next, ask God to help you allow them to experience their own journey, without your input. And last, pray for the willingness to repeat this process every time you are confronted by your desire to control what someone else is doing. It's a simple fact that the more we pray for anything, the less fear we feel. And that's our goal, after all.

✦

It's a big decision to let go of fear, and it's probably safe to say that it will never be gone entirely. But we can be at peace for spans of time when we let God take charge of our journey and everyone else's, too. Detachment is easier when we remember that God will handle the journey—everyone's journey.

# pause *and* reflect

No one becomes an expert at detachment overnight. I hope the two hundred essays in this small book, which focus again and again on a few simple ideas, presented from varying perspectives, will strengthen your resolve at making detachment a priority. The good news is that we literally have the rest of our lives to practice the behaviors that will allow us to live and let live. Many people I have come to cherish on my thirty-five-year journey consider detachment an art, which gives me hope everyday that my progress is perfect as is, and that I will arrive at my destination at the right time.

Most of us were not raised by parents who were good examples of how detachment should look. Like us, they struggled to make life work out to fit their preconceptions. And they lived with more chaos than peace. Perhaps their attempts to control us ultimately brought us here. If so, let's consider that a blessing to be grateful for. Look at the joys we are discovering.

We are becoming quite practiced at using tools that will give us peace and hope and a quiet sense of well-being.

We are learning to envision who we want to be and how we want to behave, which better prepares us for the changes we are making.

We are learning to witness for our fellow travelers, rather than giving them unwanted suggestions.

We are learning to be responsible for ourselves only, and we are becoming very adept at letting others take responsibility for themselves.

We are learning to treasure silence, knowing that our answers reside there.

We are learning the value of surrendering our need to control anyone and any situation, thus relieving ourselves of a huge and exhausting burden.

We have learned the difference between unconditional love and control, and we are becoming quite practiced at backing off, allowing others and ourselves to be free.

We have learned how attachment differs from detachment, and why one feels good and the other imprisons us.

Not letting the behavior of others control us, define us, or determine how we feel is a gift of epic proportions, a realization that changes every other aspect of our lives.

We have learned the value of prayer in changing everything about us and how we perceive the world around us. Nothing remains the same when we apply the principle of prayer.

We have learned that everyone who has crossed, is crossing, or is yet to cross our path has been called to us for the lessons that we must share. For this we can be grateful and relieved. No one is on our path uninvited.

It is my hope that the thoughts here have offered you a new way of seeing. That's all any of us can hope for if we want to experience a life that's measured by more peace. My personal goal is to enjoy more peace, more joy, and more quiet spaces in the day. All I have shared here is what I have gleaned from all the many very wise people I have traveled with. Together, we can make a difference in this world. I think that's our individual and united assignment, in fact.

Let's move forward, now, with hope and gentleness, and demonstrate for others that we can live in a state of love and companionship without binding others to us. It can be done. I am doing it. You can do it too. And never forget, angels are hovering ever so close to help us when we falter.

# Acknowledgments

THERE ARE SO MANY PEOPLE WHO COME TO MIND BUT first I want to express my gratitude to Jan Johnson, who has been a friend and supporter for many years. I appreciate her giving me the opportunity to join the team at Conari. I look forward to a long relationship there.

All my women friends in Twelve Step support groups come next to mind. They never fail to redirect my thinking when I have gotten off course, and it's that direction that is woven into the tapestry that has become this book.

I also want to thank my friends along other spiritual paths. Broadening my own journey, with their help, has deepened whatever wisdom I can lay claim to.

No one writes a book alone. Anything I have said here has been crafted with my Higher Power's help, whose presence has never left me even though I have chosen to ignore it on occasion.

I am extremely grateful to you all and to the opportunities that have resulted from our many connections.

# About the Author

KAREN CASEY is a writer and workshop facilitator for 12-step recovery. Her first book, *Each Day a New Beginning*, has sold more than three million copies. She has published twenty-eight books since then, including *Change Your Mind and Your Life Will Follow*, which was a finalist for Books for a Better Life Award. Visit her at *www.womens-spirituality.com*.

# Subject Index

The detachment meditations are numbered from 1 to 200. The numbers following the subjects below correspond to the meditation numbers in which the topic is found; they are *not* page numbers. For example, if you want to read about "Acceptance," go to meditation numbers 9, 37, and so on.

Printed in the USA
CPSIA information can be obtained
at www.ICGtesting.com
JSHW032240291023
51056JS00003B/3